Thank You, Sister!

Thank You, Sister!

Memories of Growing Up Catholic

Beverly Pangle Scott

Send all inquiries to:
bscott4@hotmail.com

First Edition — 2003
Second Edition — 2008

Printed in the United States of America

Library of Congress Control Number: 2003102328

This book is lovingly dedicated to my wonderful parents: Victor Clayton Pangle (d. 1974) and Alberta Morgan Pangle for the sacrifices they made to send four children through twelve years of Catholic schooling.

It is also dedicated in gratitude to the beloved Sisters of Charity of the Blessed Virgin Mary (BVMs) who touched my life:

Sr. Lena Cox (d. 1968)

Sr. Delrita Daly (d. 1993)

Sr. Rupertine Garlick (d. 1980)

Sr. Mary St. Roche Gorman (d. 1967)

Sr. Georgius Parks (d. 1991)

Sr. St. Camillus White (d. 1994)

Sr. Elaine Campbell (formerly Sr. Harold)

Sr. Genevieve Freund (formerly Sr. Leonine)

Sr. Catherine Hinchy (formerly Sr. Honoria)

Ms. Vivian Roney (formerly Sr. Carlice)

Several people deserve a mention of thanks for their interest in this project. I would like to thank my daughter Jessica Scott and cousin Denise Laub Frye for their constructive criticisms in the pre-editing stage of the manuscript. Also, a word of thanks goes to my husband Randall Scott and daughter Morgan Scott for all of their support. Finally, I would like to thank my editor John Sprague for his belief in my message and his work on the book.

In Memory of
John Davis

Contents

Foreword

I TOO WAS A STUDENT in the parochial system, taught by the same sisters who taught Beverly Pangle Scott when she began school. Then I entered that congregation of religious women and spent forty-seven years of my life on the other side of the desk. From both experiences I can highly recommend these reminiscences. They are a good read and will bring back many memories, not only to those from parochial schools, but to most who attended school in those less complicated times.

Ms. Scott seems to have tremendous recall, and my most common experience as I read was a rather startled, "Yes! I forgot that," and it brings a glow. I think everyone who reads this account will experience something of the same.

I also appreciate Ms. Scott's experiences as an antidote to the ruler-wielding nun of the oft-repeated stereotype (someone else's "experience," always). I never saw any sister act like that, either when I was a pupil or as a fellow teacher, in any part of my long life. The sisters I knew, like the ones Beverly Scott knew, loved their kids and did all they could for them. We still can see how lovingly the retired Sisters, even the very old and infirm, respond with delight when children come. We also see the great number of former pupils who remember "Sister" and come to see her from great distances because she taught them fifty or sixty years ago and gave them the impetus to make great strides in their later lives.

These are the kind of persons Beverly Scott remembers and shares with us. The reader is in for some enjoyable hours.

—Sister Jean Byrne, B.V.M.

BEFORE MY ENTRY into the parish school, my memories of life at church are somewhat vague. In the haze of one memory, I can see myself kneeling at Sunday Mass and still being too small to see over the top of the pew. In another fuzzy recollection, I picture myself at a Benediction service mesmerized by my father's wonderful deep voice as he stands next to me singing the beautiful Latin hymns with the rest of the congregation.

I have three very clear memories that precede my entry into grade school. In the first, it is a sunny Saturday afternoon. My dad has allowed me the privilege of going with him to help with the preparations for a church picnic to be held that evening. When we arrive, many men are already present preparing the barbecue to be served. A man named Ralph Mahoney walks up to greet Daddy and me. He offers my dad a cold beer. My father accepts and, as he pulls the bottle out of the icy water of the washtub, I notice that it is a familiar brown bottle of Falstaff beer. Knowing our routine at home, in a coy manner, I ask Daddy if I might have the first sip. Along with Mr. Mahoney, Daddy chuckles and then lets me take a miniscule taste. The rest of the day is spent blissfully with Daddy as the finishing touches are added to make this benefit picnic a success.

In the second experience, Mom, Dad, and I are leaving Sunday Mass. We have to wait a few minutes because my older brother has to change out of his altar boy garments. Daddy suggests that we walk down and look at the new gymnasium that has just recently been completed. (The proceeds from the summer picnic had helped with the funding for this building.) I am four years old and this gym is the largest building I have ever seen. Our voices echo as we stand inside and talk about the structure. The floor of the new basketball court is gleaming and begging me to walk across it. At the moment I take a step, my dad stops me and explains that my shoes have hard soles and that they could damage the new floor. Then he looks across the floor to the stage and says, "Beverly, someday you will be on that stage and I will be so proud of you."

In the third scene, which I vividly recall, it is a late spring evening and the whole family is at the church. After attending a ceremony, Mom and I are standing outside talking to two of the nuns. Mother is asking them about their plans for the summer, and then she mentions that I will be starting school there in the fall. With the attention now on me, I bury my face in the folds of Mom's skirt. One of the sisters asks me a question and I respond in a barely audible voice. Then Mother does what all parents do and live to regret. She asks me to "perform." She tells the sisters that I know the "Hail Mary" and then she tells me to say it for them. Feeling uncomfortable, I squirm and demur. Thankfully, the younger nun looks kindly at me and says, "Oh, I'm sure you do know all of your prayers, Beverly. I look forward to seeing you and hearing them next fall when you come to school." I am instantly relieved. This is my first inkling of the gratitude I will feel for these wonderful women.

"To this day I cannot adequately describe the impact Sister Carlice's words had on me."

EXCITEMENT CAME in the form of two postcards that summer of 1955. The first gave me the opportunity to celebrate my sixth birthday on "Chickarooni," a children's afternoon television show. The second postcard was an invitation to visit room 102 at Our Lady of Perpetual Help Catholic School in the fall. My first-grade teacher would be Sister Carlice, and I was very curious. Although I did not know who she was, my older brother did, and he and Mom told me that Sister was young, pretty, and sweet.

I walked into Sister Carlice's room on the first day of school, arriving late for some reason. Everyone else was already in a seat and the class was just getting ready to say the Hail Mary. As I entered, every eye was on me. Sister smiled in greeting and said, "Oh, you are just in time to say prayers. Let us see if you can find your desk. You are in the fifth seat of the second row." I do not know whether it was because I was shy or just did not know how to count, but I started hesitantly down one aisle. A girl smiled up at me and pointed to the desk behind her saying, "Here's where you sit!" Her name was Suzanne Sims. I will never forget her because she was so sweet and helpful. It was a relief to sit down and have the focus off me.

Taped to my desktop with my name printed on it was a pink strip of paper. There was a slot for a pencil and underneath the seat, space for books and supplies. On the walls above the two chalkboards were the letters of the alphabet printed on posters, in both upper and lower case. Above these posters on the sidewall of the classroom were two long, rectangular boxes with sheet metal curved inward. These would soon fascinate me. Occasionally, someone would flip the wrong wall switch and these boxes would glow with a beautiful, violet color. Apparently, they were ultraviolet lights, which had been installed many years earlier, possibly in an attempt to control the spread of tuberculosis.

My mom had left the room as soon as I had found my seat, and Sister Carlice told us to stand to say the Hail Mary. The rest of the morning is a blur. I do remember that we got our first worksheet. It was a picture of a large ball with a single stripe going around the middle of it. We were directed to take out a blue crayon and a red crayon. Then we were told to color the ball blue and the stripe red. Although I usually loved to color and could do a good job, this time I must have rushed. When I later showed the paper to mom, she pointed out in a kind way that I had colored outside the lines and that I usually did better. This made an impression on me, and established in my mind expectations of doing my best.

I don't remember much more about that day except that I immediately loved Sister Carlice. I also remember that I had a horrible cold that day and I was somewhat miserable.

Thankfully, we got out of school early on the first day. Afterward, my mom, brothers, and a neighboring family went on a picnic at a place on the lake called Camp Columbus.

ONE OF MY EARLIEST memories from our first full days of school was morning recess. I had met and instantly fallen in love with a new friend named Catherine. Our admiration was mutual and we became inseparable. We just seemed to be curiously connected, and definitely felt that we had known each other all of our short lives. On this particular day, we were outside during the first short recess. Within some shrubbery, we had discovered a cozy little hideaway—just big enough for two little girls to sit and play house. Completely absorbed in our imaginary world, we hadn't noticed that Sister had rung the hand bell until suddenly Richie Wilbanks, one of our classmates, came running toward us screaming, "You two are in big trouble! Sister sent me out here to find you!"

When we got to the classroom, we were mortified to have to face Sister, especially in front of the whole class. Looking back, I realize that Sister Carlice was terrified, fearing that we had walked away, or worse. She questioned us as to where we had been and then sternly told us to pay closer attention in the future. I remember that, more than having her scold us, I regretted having let her down. Both Catherine and I were extremely conscientious, and it was humiliating to have failed in this way.

I was a child who suffered from severe separation anxiety. Leaving my mother each day was agony. For this reason, I was very often "sick." It was not that I was faking. I either really made myself sick from nervousness, or I did not tolerate well minor illnesses such as a cold. In any event, my absences were frequent. Even so, I caught on quickly and had no trouble keeping up with my work. Moreover, I adored Sister Carlice.

Soon after we began school, Sister put us into reading groups. We were "angels" of various colors, according to our ability. I am sure I was a pink angel. Although that was not the low reading group, I always wanted to be in the low group because I liked their color better. This was just a little way that Sister kept us from being proud about our reading status. She made all of the colors sound so desirable that each child wished she were in some other group.

When Sister talked to us about religion, she took on a luminous quality. When she spoke of sanctifying grace or heaven, I could see the most wonderful colors and taste the most delicious flavors. To this day, I cannot adequately describe the incredible impact her words had on my life. I just knew from the time I heard her speak about these things that I wanted to be so very good all my life. I did not want to miss the rewards of God's love.

Some days, we would find an easel sitting in the front of the classroom. Hanging on the easel was a collection of prints depicting various scenes from the Bible. These were large pictures arranged on a string much like a calendar so that the pages could be flipped and only one would be showing. My heart leapt for joy whenever this easel was set up because I knew it meant Sister Carlice would be telling us a story about the picture.

Many of the stories have stuck with me and probably will forever. She made the story of Lazarus and Dives come alive. With that story, she nurtured the seed of compassion that my parents had already implanted within me. When she told the story of the Prodigal Son, I realized the pain of the Father and silently vowed never to hurt my parents or our heavenly Father by turning away from them. The wedding feast at Cana brought a glimmer of anticipation for my First Communion, which I would make in second grade. Finally, the stories of the Good Shepherd and Jesus surrounded by the little children made me long to talk to him in prayer. The picture and story of Jesus as a boy of twelve teaching the elders in the synagogue made me want to learn about God and serve his will.

Sister was equally wonderful when she taught us new prayers. I particularly loved the *Morning Offering*. She explained so beautifully how God had freely given us life and how we could offer back every aspect of our lives every day. Each morning we sang the beautiful song that Bishop Sheen had composed, "Lovely Lady Dressed in Blue." In those ways, Sister helped us to form images of Jesus at all stages of his life. Through the song, we saw him sitting on his mother's lap. She used the story of Jesus in the temple at twelve to show us that, even when he was a child, he was obedient to God. We saw him as our friend and our Savior, and by the end of the year, we began to open our eyes to his divinity.

As first graders, we did not immediately receive the dark blue *Baltimore Catechism*. Instead, we had a little simplified version that I believe Sister had made. It had a pink paper cover and inside were dittoed pages of questions and answers about God. It began with the familiar questions

"Who made you?" "Who is God?" and "Why did God make you?" Because my brother was four years older and had already learned them, I was quite familiar with these questions. I can remember feeling so grown up when it came my turn to learn the answers.

OUR SCHOOL DAY was permeated with reminders of God and his goodness. Sister took every opportunity to point out the gratitude we should each have for what we had been given. Examples would include our parents, our food, our learning opportunities, our friends, and so on. Out of all of those, I particularly remember the discussions regarding our parents' sacrifices to send us to a Catholic school. By the time Sister would finish, I would want to run home and hug my parents. This is an essential link to the success of my grade-school experience. Parents were not the enemy. It was assumed that they were filled with God's love and grace. As such, they were presumed to have their children's best interest at heart.

One of the most comforting prayers I learned that year was the prayer to the Guardian Angel. When I made my way down the aisle to my seat on that first day, I looked up and saw a most beautiful picture. High on the wall in the back of the classroom was that exquisite picture of the guardian angel protecting the little boy and girl as they walked across a dilapidated bridge. I have never seen a rendering of that print quite as lovely as the one in Sister Carlice's classroom. That picture became a great source of consolation to me during that year as I learned to separate from my mother. Learning the prayer reinforced the idea that I could call on my guardian angel any time I needed spiritual assistance.

The bridge the children were crossing came to symbolize for me the journey of faith across the chasm of unbelief.

Sister Carlice was an incredible teacher, but she was also great fun. From the very beginning, she delighted us by joining in games during recess. She played circle games such as "drop the handkerchief" and "hokey pokey." She even taught us one called "Little Sally Saucer." I think she truly captured our hearts when she joined us in jump rope. I remember her doing "Teddy Bear, Teddy Bear" and several of the "Cinderella dressed in . . ." routines. She even played jump rope "school" with us.

Sister was playful, but she was not a pushover. She expected us to be quiet in the classroom, and she expected us to keep our appearance and our desk neat. Every six weeks, our pastor, Father Bush, handed out report cards to each class. Wanting everything to look just right, Sister would always do a little inspection before these visits. Because the visits occurred late in the afternoon, Sister would comment on several disheveled students. She would call the person by name and say, "Tuck in your shirt (or blouse). You look like the 'wreck of the Hesperus.' " It was probably a dozen years before I learned what that meant. It did not matter that I did not completely understand the reference. It was totally clear what Sister was saying, and I never wanted to be one of those messy-looking students.

WE LEARNED A LOT about hospitality in first grade. Anytime an adult came to the door, we jumped out of our seats and verbally greeted them. We then quietly stood there until Sister finished her business with that person or until we were given permission to sit. During the time we were standing, if someone talked or squirmed, we felt we had let Sister down and behaved rudely. However, if we were on our best behavior, we would beam when the "guest" made a positive comment about us. If it were a priest at the door, Sister would ask him to give us a blessing. We would quickly kneel and cross ourselves, feeling very privileged. This attentiveness to small courtesies amazes me as I look back. We valued politeness and we were grateful for kindness shown to us, rather than thinking about them as entitlements.

Another lesson in hospitality came with our occasional classroom visitor, Sissy Ekland. Sissy was in kindergarten and her mom would sometimes work as a substitute teacher. Kindergarten was only a half-day. This meant that when Mrs. Ekland was substituting, Sissy needed a place to spend the afternoon. Sister Carlice gladly volunteered our room and we were always on our best behavior when she was there. We all thought that Sissy was adorable. I remember that she usually wore her hair in braids with little hat barrettes on the ends. I particularly remember two dresses that she wore. One of the dresses was yellow and the other was blue. They were rayon with a crinoline petticoat underneath. Sister often commented on how well behaved Sissy was and marveled that she was only in kindergarten. These comments did not make us jealous. We loved Sissy and since we were the "big" first graders, we just wanted to be good examples for her.

Because I was a very well-behaved student, I did not think much about discipline, except to think I did not want to be on the receiving end of a reprimand. It was not that there was anything horrible that would happen. I just knew that I would feel extremely humiliated if I ever broke the rules and was caught. Being caught was the weak part of that idea because I was not about to test it by breaking any rules. Nevertheless, some in my class were not so inclined as I. Now and then, someone, usually a boy, would act up. Sister Carlice would give the little criminal multiple chances and finally, in exasperation, she might have him stand in the front of the room or in front of one of the cloakroom doors. Although this sounds like a mild punishment, I knew more than one little guy to bawl his eyes out while enduring this.

On some occasions, the class as a whole would get a bit rowdy. Again, Sister would persist in her efforts to quiet us, before finally resorting to more drastic measures. This would usually occur at the end of the school day. Losing her patience, Sister would say, "All right, class, put your hands on your heads and sit there in complete silence!" What seemed like an eternity would pass and then she would dismiss us row by row to the cloakroom to get our things while we remained in total silence. When everyone was ready, we would say our prayer to the Guardian Angel, and then very somberly she would line us up to leave for the day.

On the morning following one of these group punishments, I vividly remember Sister revealing her vulnerability. After the bell rang for school to begin and we had said our morning prayers, she told us she wanted to talk to us. It went something like this:

"Class, yesterday when I went home to the convent, I looked in the mirror and I was very surprised. Do you know why?"

All of us shook our heads and said, “No, Sister.” We could tell by the tone of her voice that she was about to tell us something very, very serious.

“Well,” she continued. “I was surprised because I had expected to see an old bear in that mirror. Do you know why?”

By this time we were mesmerized and slowly shook our heads, no, again.

“I expected to see an old bear because when I got through fussing at you children yesterday, I felt like an old bear.”

You could almost feel the sadness in the room. We had been the ones at fault. We would not be quiet. Now she was telling us she felt guilty! No, this was too much for us. Our sweet Sister Carlice could not take on our guilt. I do not remember what the class as a whole said or did, but I do know she hit the mark with me. My conscientious nature went into overdrive. I would never give that woman a second’s trouble. In fact, I would do everything I could to make up for the trouble that anyone else might cause. I really think that most of us felt that way about hurting Sister Carlice. We wanted her to see the angel we saw when she looked at herself in the mirror, not an old bear.

Sister Carlice was ebullient, but very gentle. When she was peeved with one of us, the harshest thing she ever said was to refer to us as “featherhead.” Although I never aspired to that title, I do think that some of the more adventurous students actively sought it.

Sister did have one pet peeve. She would not tolerate thumbsucking. Since I did not engage in the activity, I was never the target, but I am almost positive that it was Sister

Carlice who taught us the little ditty "Baby, baby, suck your thumb. Wash your hair in bubblegum." It was my impression that the class as a whole took this chiding good-naturedly. It would probably not pass the censors today.

Although I did not suck my thumb, I did bite my fingernails to the quick. Sister was ever so gentle in her attempt to break me of that habit. I suppose she realized how nervous I was, and did not want to exacerbate the situation by humiliation of any sort. Instead, she called me up to her desk and talked to me about it. She told me that my little hands would look so pretty if I did not bite my nails, and then she challenged me. She told me that if I could quit biting my nails for six weeks, she would give me a prize. I really put my heart into the task and actually made progress. Unfortunately, six weeks was a very long time to a six-year-old. At some point, I went back to the old habit. However, Sister was compassionate. She noted my good effort and gave me my prize anyway. It was a little beige, plastic statue of the Blessed Virgin.

ALONG WITH the many reminders of our parents' goodness, the nuns frequently reinforced in our minds the faith of those we were able to observe. For instance, it would be pointed out to us that many parishioners went to daily Mass. These people were used to illustrate examples of faith in action. One person that I particularly remember was a man named Mr. Leland. He was at the 8:00 A.M. Mass every day. One of his two beautiful daughters temporarily taught at Our Lady of Perpetual Help (OLPH). Those of us who knew her were thrilled when she confided in us that she would be joining a convent. We could practically see a halo above her head! All of these years later, I still think of Mr. Leland and the impact his example of faith had on me. I frequently pray that his glory in heaven be increased because of his powerful influence. However, I wonder if I would have really known what a treasure he was if the nuns had not pointed it out to me.

Just as we saw the goodness of others, we were reminded many times of the example that we should show through our actions. Repeatedly it was reinforced that we should especially be aware of this with regard to our behavior around non-Catholics. We were not encouraged to proselytize, but rather to evangelize through our conduct. Living the Gospel message was emphasized much more than memorizing it. This is not to say that understanding scripture was not important. We were inundated with biblical truths throughout our school day. These precepts permeated our lives and usually we did not even realize they were scriptural in origin. It is true that as I got older my lack of a repertoire of biblical quotations put me behind in some discussions with non-Catholics. At the same time, when I did venture on my own to really read and study Scripture, I realized how richly steeped in its truths I already was.

It seemed that every event in first grade was an opportunity for excitement. Christmas was no exception. We learned about Advent, and at home had our own Advent wreath. Actually, we had always (as far as I know) had an Advent wreath. The thing that was different about the wreath that year was that Mom used white candles that had glitter on them! It was not that she planned it that way. By that time, she and Daddy had three children, and they were in the process of planning and building a new house. I know she probably did not have time for an Advent wreath that year, but I came home from school very excited and I insisted that we have one. I wanted us to kneel around it every night and say the rosary the way we had done before.

Mom did not resist my pleas, but she did not have time to buy the traditional three blue/purple candles and one pink one. All she had handy were the aforementioned glitter candles. I protested, but she assured me it was okay, and she made the wreath. It is such a good example of the cycle that went on in Catholic schools. Good parents wanting good religious education for their children would sacrifice in order to send them to be taught by the nuns. The children would become spiritually fed and then go home and insist on reinforcement of this nourishment through religious practices there.

Preparing for the Christmas program at school was a major undertaking. The teachers wanted it to be just right. It always consisted of a live nativity scene with a retelling of the gospel story of the birth of Christ. Each class would be assigned to stand and sing a particular Christmas carol at the appropriate time. In Sister Carlice's class, the carol was "O Come, Little Children." I had never heard this song before and I immediately fell in love with it. Of course, as luck would have it, I caught an awful cold just before the performance and missed both the performance and the class Christmas party. When I came back to school after the Christmas break, there in my desk was the goody bag from the party with the most humongous peppermint stick I had ever seen. I did not even particularly like peppermint, but I made sure to gloat over this treasure as my older brother and I rode the bus home that afternoon.

AT SOME POINT in the school year, the annual magazine drive came around. My older brother who was in fifth grade made a rule: Only the older of the two kids in school would be allowed to sell the subscriptions. He reasoned that eventually I would get my turn when he went on to high school and my younger brother began first grade. To make this rule more acceptable to me he promised that I could pick out a prize of my choice that resulted from the sales he generated. I looked at the little prize brochure and eyeing some of the treasures, decided I was getting the better end of the deal.

He went on to be a super salesman, and after doing none of the work, I smugly selected a set of beautiful colored pencils. They came in a plastic case. You could slide back the lid on the case and it would become a base so that the pencils could be displayed upright. Proudly, I took the pencils to school and set them up on my desk. Sister Carlice was very tolerant of the pencils until they began to create a mild stir. It seemed that every student who sat near me wanted to borrow one of the pretty pencils. Finally, Sister had had enough, and she declared the pencils banned from the classroom. She was not mean about it, but she was exasperated by the semichaos they caused.

A few days later, my brother was absent from school. I received a message from Sister Delrita that I was to go to her classroom at the end of the day. The combination of being shy and being terrified of her made me panic-stricken. Cautiously, I knocked on the door to her classroom. The class was standing for the prayer at the end of the day, and a student admitted me into the room. Sister beamed at me and said she had something that she wanted me to give to my brother. It was a beautiful statue of St. Joseph. Sister told me to tell him it was a special gift for the good job he had done selling magazines.

She could not have known what a gift she had given to me. Her example made me begin to realize that a person cannot be boxed in to fit just one category. Sister had the reputation for being stern and it was well deserved, but she was also kind and thoughtful and after my experience with her, I knew she was probably many more things. I just had not discovered everything about her. It was my first inkling that we never fully know others; therefore, we should not judge them.

I approached the season of Lent seriously for the first time that year. When I was five, I had been the family clown, declaring that for Lent I would give up watermelon and beer! However, in first grade I really wanted to make a sacrifice for Our Lord. I do not remember what I gave up that year, but I know it was very likely candy. I also know that I would have tried hard to live up to the sacrifice. It was during the primary grades that I developed a true sorrow for the passion and death of our Lord.

When I thought about those events, the agony in the garden would most often come to my mind. Sister had described to us the weight of our sins on the blameless Jesus. She was very clear that the distress he was experiencing at that time was so excruciating that his sweat contained blood. I pictured him as he had been depicted, kneeling against the boulder in the garden, feeling totally alone as the disciples slept nearby. I wanted more than anything to console him, and if my little Lenten sacrifice could demonstrate that desire, I was more than willing to endure it.

At school, I remember going to Mass and proudly receiving the ashes on my forehead. I felt so privileged to be Catholic. I was careful all day not to brush my hand across my forehead and perhaps remove some of the ashes. We vaguely understood that those ashes symbolized the dust we came from, but mostly we identified receiving the ashes with joining ourselves to Christ's suffering as the Lenten season began.

As the Easter break approached, we began to get excited about secular things. The girls were shopping for Easter dresses, and the boys would get new suits. The prospect of dyeing Easter eggs was something I looked forward to with great anticipation. One day, about a week before we got out of school for the holiday, Sister explained to us that if we finished all of our work, we would do something very special that afternoon. Of course, we did and so our project began. We made little Easter baskets out of construction paper.

Looking back, I think Sister must have been able to work magic. She took this simple task of making the baskets and somehow stretched it out for days. There was really nothing to them. We each took a piece of the paper she had prepared, which had four lines drawn on it. Two horizontally divided the page and two vertically divided the page into thirds. We then took our scissors and followed Sister's instructions as to where on the lines to cut. Next, we brought the ends up to form the basket and she came around and put a staple on each side to hold it all together. We cut a strip of construction paper for the handle, and then cut out two construction paper tulips she had drawn for us. These went on either side of the handle. That was it, but we did all this bit by bit. Only if we behaved and got our work done would we get to proceed. It really elevated this simple undertaking to something very thrilling.

On the last day of school before the break, the baskets were ready at last. We put them on our desks and went to lunch. When we returned after recess, much to our horror, they were gone! Sister was beside herself. She sent me to tell Sister Honoria and Sister Delrita, and she sent other students to tell other teachers. No one knew what had happened, but each one was sympathetic. Sorrowfully, we began our afternoon tasks. Finally, Sister said that she was going to give us an afternoon recess as a treat to make up for the lost baskets. We went outside with very heavy hearts.

When we returned to the classroom fifteen or twenty minutes later, there were our baskets back on our desks, but with a difference. Each was filled with Easter grass and candy! We could not believe it. I could have sworn that I saw tears of joy in Sister's eyes. Again, she sent me and the other messengers to tell all of the teachers our wonderful news. I can still see the bemused expressions on Sisters Honoria and Delrita's faces as I excitedly told them about our visit from the Easter Bunny. I still cannot believe how convincing Sister Carlice had been as she displayed her distress over the "loss" of the baskets. Her willingness to give us this delightful memory is something that continues to stir gratitude within me.

ON THE EVE of the last school day in April, Sister made an announcement. Just before dismissal, Sister told us that there would be a surprise when we got back to school the next morning. I could not imagine what it would be. When I walked into the classroom the next day, I was almost breathless. There had always been a colorful statue of Mary on a pedestal in the front of the classroom. Now what we saw there was a most beautiful tribute to the Blessed Mother. The statue, which was about two feet high, had been placed on a table. The table was covered with pale blue taffeta under pale blue gathered netting. Beautiful satin bows adorned the corners. Behind the table and beginning about six feet above it, hung a curtain of the taffeta and net.

The effect was stunning. After the "oohs and ahs" settled down, Sister explained to us that May is the month set aside by the Church to honor Mary. She told us that we could bring flowers from our gardens to adorn her display. She also took that time to explain carefully that we do not worship or adore Mary, but we do honor her for saying "yes" so completely to God.

I went home that day and insisted that my mom let me use my desk in my bedroom for a beautiful display to honor the Blessed Virgin. Poor Mom, as if she did not have enough to do, but still she granted my request. Of course, I did not have a statue of equivalent size, but I did have a beautiful framed print of Mary and I used that as my centerpiece.

Of all the classrooms with these Mary "altars," I thought ours was the prettiest. I also thought that honoring Mary in this way was wonderful. Imagine my joy when I heard about the all-school May procession. Hearing horror stories about Catholic schools has always made me cringe. Sometimes I wonder if most of the stories have not evolved from the preparation for events such as a May procession. It was during practices for these events that the nuns seemed tense. In reality, they desperately wanted to preserve the dignity and solemnity of the particular event, and they wanted us to make it as perfect a gift as possible. I never minded the tedious rehearsals and the occasional sharp words. I look at the slovenly way many serious celebrations are carried out today, and I would give anything to have Sister Whoever in charge again.

A most amazing thing happened regarding my first May procession. Each year one of the eighth-grade girls was selected to crown the large outdoor statue of Mary with a wreath of fresh flowers. A first-grade boy carried the crown on a satin pillow, and there were four long, satin ribbons attached to each of the four corners. Two girls from each of the two first-grade classes would carry one of the streamers. Sister picked me as one of the girls from our class. Kathy was the other girl's name, and I have no memory of the students selected from the other class. I could not believe I had been chosen for this. My mom made me a gorgeous floor-length pale-blue dress that had two ruffled medallions on the front. I think all four of the streamer carriers must have been required to wear pale blue because I do not remember any other color being worn.

The day of the procession finally arrived. It was a Sunday and everyone was supposed to be in his or her classroom about thirty minutes before it started. My Mom had fixed my long hair in sausage curls and the dress was very pretty. When I came into the school building, I saw Sister Carlice in the hall talking to one of the other nuns. I looked way down to the other end of the hall and saw the elder brother of

Carol Drake, one of my friends. This boy was in seventh or eighth grade and he seemed like an adult compared to me. When he saw me, he stretched out his arms and called to me. I hurried to him and when I got there, he bent down and lifted me high in the air and said, "You look so beautiful, just like a little angel." He kissed me gently on the cheek and slowly lowered me to the floor. It was one of the tenderest moments in my life. I think about it often because it was a moment of pure gift for me from someone who could just as well have told me to get lost.

I strain to know what it was that gave this twelve-or thirteen-year-old boy the humility and the fortitude to do such a kind thing. I had never had a conversation with him before. We knew each other because he and his sister rode my school bus, but that does not explain his unabashed expression of affection. His family moved away the next year. I have often wondered what happened to him. I like to imagine that he grew up to have a loving family himself, and from time to time I ask God to bless him for his thoughtfulness to me so long ago.

I was completely hooked on devotion to Mary after my first May procession. The songs we sang were beautiful, and later I would constantly sing them at home. We recited the wonderful Litany of Loretto, which listed the various titles conferred on Mary by the Church. All eyes were on the chosen eighth-grade girl as she lovingly placed the crown of flowers on the head of the statue. We knew this statue represented the Mother of Jesus, and we were beginning to understand why "All generations will call me blessed."

The culmination of this event was Benediction, a ceremony to worship the Triune God. This was absolutely fitting since honoring Mary always leads us to the adoration of her Son, Jesus. Throughout my years in grade school, I felt privileged to participate in this as well as other Church-related events. The May procession was held outside, and I always hoped that as many non-Catholics as possible would pass by on the busy street and see our devotion.

Now that my love for Mary had been firmly established, imagine my delight to think that my birthday came during the Blessed Mother's month. A few years later, I was nearly delirious to discover that May 31, my actual birthday, was set aside by the Church as the feast of the Queenship of Mary. (This date is now set aside to honor the Visitation of Mary to her cousin Elizabeth. The Feast of the Queenship of Mary was moved to August.) Then, a lifetime later, I would feel so very privileged when my first daughter would be born on the feast of the Immaculate Conception, and my second daughter would be born on October 13. This day is significant because it was on that day in 1917 that Mary appeared for the last time to the three shepherd children in Fatima, Portugal, and the miracle of the sun occurred before a crowd of 70,000 people.

DURING MY YEARS in grade school, exams were given each semester to the students in grades four through eight. These exams were made up at the diocesan office in Nashville, and produced great anxiety among the students. Because they were viewed seriously, and to reduce the amount of distraction as much as possible, grades one, two, and three were allowed to start summer vacation a week early. I gloated over this to my older brother as he struggled with the dreaded exams.

Since my birthday was the last day in May, I asked my mom if I could invite all of the girls in my class to my party. She readily said yes, but I had yet one more request. I wanted Sister Carlice to be at my party. Nuns were not allowed to go anywhere alone. When my mom spoke to Sister, it was decided that she would come and in order to fulfill the rules, Sister Delrita would accompany her.

My father took off work early in order to pick up the two nuns and bring them to my party. It was one of my biggest thrills and far exceeded the joy of any presents I received that day. Sister gave me a little plaque. It had an irregular

Sisters Mary Carlice and Mary Delrita attend Beverly's party on her seventh birthday.

shape, which was about five inches across at its widest point. In the center was a pewter medallion, which I believe portrayed the crucifixion. Surrounding that was ornate, lacey clear plastic. There was a piece of clear plastic in the back that pulled out to serve as a stand. I saved this treasure for many years until it finally got broken. The party was an incredible end to my wonderful first year of school.

Chapter Two

"Second grade was very special because this was the year we made our First Confession and First Holy Communion."

DURING THE TWELVE YEARS of my Catholic schooling, I was fortunate to attend schools that were staffed mostly with nuns. Occasionally, a slot would be filled by a lay teacher, and that was the case for my second-grade experience. Before school began that year, I could not imagine being taught by anyone other than Sister Carlice. This all changed on the very first day of school when Virginia Skelton walked into the classroom. She was very young and incredibly sweet. She wore the most beautiful pair of glasses. They had metallic, mauve-colored rims.

Miss Skelton seemed to love teaching. Unfortunately, her first year at Our Lady of Perpetual Help was also her last. I don't really know what happened, but I do know that she caught every little illness that her students could possibly pass along to her. She missed almost as many days as I did. Mom always thought that must have played a part in her leaving. Whatever her reasons for not returning the following year, while we had her as our teacher, we loved her.

Miss Skelton especially loved the girls. Being a first-year teacher, she undoubtedly found our undying loyalty and willingness to cooperate a blessing. We loved it when she would come up with a new seating chart because she always made us feel so special if she put us in the front. Of course, during the school year, this happened to us all, and no one was left out.

Second grade was very special because this was the year we made our First Confession and First Holy Communion. When a lay teacher taught a class, it was customary for one of the nuns to come in to teach religion. Imagine our delight when our beloved Sister Carlice came to our room for this purpose. She lovingly prepared us for reception of the Eucharist. The gift that Jesus had left us of his body and blood was more special than anything else in life. Sister emphasized the care we should take to make certain our souls were spotless. She impressed upon us what a privilege it was to receive Holy Communion.

Over a period of about six weeks, we learned all about the Eucharist and Confession. Additionally, Father Bush met with us in the church and quizzed us orally to see if we had acquired the necessary knowledge and disposition to receive Our Lord for the first time. During one visit to the church, Sister let us enter the confessional and experience what it would be like to kneel there behind the curtain. Yes, at that time there was only a curtain over the cubicles on each side of the priest. When the day finally came to make our first Confession, it was comical when some students entered the confessional and spoke in a normal, street voice. Invariably these were the very students who apparently were a little overzealous and who would recite a litany of minor infractions that were hardly sinful. Those of us in the pews outside would quietly shake with laughter as the drivel rolled on within reach of our ears.

DURING FIRST and second grades, we periodically received colorful, Catholic booklets called *MINE* magazine. I always disliked the name of these periodicals, but I loved getting them. Mom had inundated our house with children's magazines when I was preschool age, and I had looked forward each month to the upcoming issues. Receiving *MINE* magazine seemed like a natural link to my home and gave me a cozy feeling. The name irritated me because even though I had not yet officially learned grammar rules, for me to say "I got my *MINE* magazine today," grated on my nerves, as it seemed to me to be inappropriate usage.

The magazine itself was great. It usually had a wonderful story and I particularly remember one that we read around the time of our First Communion preparation. It told about a young boy who lived during the time of the persecutions of the early church. Someone older was charged with the responsibility of carrying the Eucharist to a group of Christians some distance away, but something prevented him from doing it at the time. With no one else available, the young boy stepped forward and volunteered. Although it was a dangerous mission, the boy was not afraid. Predictably, he was set upon by vicious attackers, but was able to consume the sacred hosts before he died.

This story made quite an impression on me. I wanted to value the Eucharist as sincerely as did that young boy. I did not think that I would ever have to give my life to defend it, but I vaguely understood that there were other sacrifices that I could accept that would demonstrate my own sincerity.

About a week before the First Communion Mass, we began to practice processing into church, filing into the pews, and then actually going up to and kneeling at the altar railing. Just before practice was over on the last day, we received a wonderful surprise. The girls got a white, patent leather purse. It contained a beautiful white rosary and a little white missal. On the inside cover of this prayer book was a crucifix made of a mother-of-pearl-like material. It had been glued to a gold foil background. The boys each received a black rosary and their prayer books had black covers. Each of us received a card with a beautiful picture of Pope Pius X. This saint was responsible for assuring that children who had reached the age of reason could receive Communion. The card had a little white tassel hanging from it and inside there was a place to write pertinent information about our First Communion day.

We made our First Communion on a Sunday in October at the eight o'clock Mass. At that time, we had to fast after midnight in order to take Communion. It was difficult not to eat or drink anything, but I think we all felt very willing to make this sacrifice in order to receive Jesus in this special way. After Mass, all of us gathered on the steps in front of the school gymnasium for a picture. Father Bush was also in the picture with us. I remember the morning was very cool, but it was a beautiful, sunny day.

Second grade brought me no relief regarding separation from my mother. One day I told Miss Skelton that I was sick to my stomach. She asked if I would like to call my mother

Beverly in her First Communion dress kneeling before a picture of the Virgin Mary.

and go home. What a novel idea! I didn't know that this was a possibility. I nodded, and she sent me across the hall to the office. On the way back to the classroom, I ran into Sister Carlice, who asked me what was wrong. When I told her, she suggested that she take me through the doorway to the convent and let me try sipping on a Coke. I couldn't believe the attention and I told her that would be fine.

The housekeeper got me a Coke in one of those little six-ounce bottles, which we were convinced back then tasted better, and I slowly drank it. I reveled in the fact that I was in the nuns' actual home. Soon I forgot all about the upset stomach, but my dad had already been called, so I gleefully went home for the day. Upon arriving there and being dropped off by my father, I convinced Mom to let me walk to an aunt's house to spend the afternoon. Aunt Lucille and I then watched "The Edge of Night" to find out what was happening to Mike Carr, her favorite character. Afterward, she taught me how to embroider. It had been a very good day.

My little adventure had been exciting, and it had momentarily taken my mind off missing Mom. Unfortunately, the euphoria did not last and so I decided to try this trick again. Just as had happened the first time, Miss Skelton sent me across the hall to the office. Similarly, I ran into Sister Carlice, but this time she was not quite as solicitous. She frowned and asked me where I was going. I gave my most pathetic look, and explained that I was feeling sick and I was going to call my father to pick me up. She let me know right away that I was not going to make a habit of this and told me I should go back to class and try to "stick it out" until the end of the day.

I must have looked pitiful because she retreated slightly from her stance and said that maybe the housekeeper could give me some soda and crackers to ease my stomach. I brightened at this, but quickly changed. There was no Coke in the six-ounce bottle this time. There was only Seven-Up. This was not good! Because Mom had always used Seven-Up to settle her stomach, I regarded it as medicine, and I detested the stuff! Out of politeness, I choked down a glassful, but never again (during second grade) did I feign a stomachache.

EACH YEAR AT SCHOOL, there were particular prayers or songs that I grew to love. However, during the summer just before second grade, my cousin Denise taught me a special prayer one night just before I went to sleep. It was called "Help Me, Dear God." I was thrilled upon receiving my little First Communion missal to find that this prayer was in it. To this day, I sometimes recite this prayer and I am instantly reminded of my spiritual goals. The lyrical quality of the verses that I loved so much as a child sound a bit sing/song today, but the message is pure. I include it here:

Help me, Dear God
To live the way
You want me to live
Day by day.

Oh show me how
To please you best
When I'm at work
Or play or rest.

And may I often
Think of you,
And never say
What isn't true.

And never do
What isn't right.
I think that's all
Dear God, goodnight.

Academically, most of second grade was a review of concepts we had learned in first grade. It was a more relaxing year. This was providential because in October my family moved into a new house. I got my own room and I felt like the richest little girl in the world. Daddy let me pick out the paint color for my walls and I chose orchid. It did not matter to me that I slept on an old studio couch and had a very old dresser and chest of drawers as my furniture. As far as I was concerned, my room was beautiful.

As if Mom did not have enough to do with rearing three children and moving into a brand new house, she was also pregnant. The baby was due in January. All of this excitement made for a very joyful time in my family, and our first Christmas in the new house was particularly happy.

As the middle of January arrived, so did my sister, Mary Elaine. Mom was in the hospital four or five days with her, and then we had about a week and a half of relative calm. One evening, when Mary Elaine was two weeks old, my dad got home from work and wanted to hold her for a while. Things seemed fine when suddenly he told Mom that something was wrong. Mary Elaine had stopped breathing! Mother took the still infant from Daddy and told him to call our pediatrician. She then tried to revive her, unsuccessfully at first. She ran over to the nearby bathroom sink and sprinkled some water on Mary Elaine's forehead and began saying the words of Baptism. At that instant, Mary began breathing again. In the meantime, Daddy had reached the doctor who told him to rush the baby to the hospital where he would meet them. A neighbor came over and sat with us through the long hours as we waited for word. Finally, my younger brother and I had to go to bed.

My dad awakened me the next morning. He told me that Mary Elaine had double pneumonia. She had a very high fever, and the doctors were doing everything they could for her. He told me that she would probably be in the hospital for a while. More important, he told me that Mother would be staying there with her. By now I had bonded a little with this new baby, but I was glued to my mother. The news that she would be away from home was devastating to me.

My dad tried his best that morning to brush out the tangles in my very long hair. It was exasperating for him since I was quite tender-headed. I went to school looking a little less neat than usual, but outwardly, probably no one would have guessed about the turmoil of the previous night. No one, that is, except Sister Carlice. Miss Skelton sent me to Sister's classroom with a note about some unrelated matter. I was to wait for an answer.

When Sister handed me her reply, she asked me how the new baby was doing. I was almost out the door and being polite and shy, I did not want to dillydally. I quickly said, "Oh, she's fine, Sister." When I got to the hall, I remembered the events of the night before. I ran back into her classroom and blurted, "Oh, Sister, my new baby sister is really sick and almost died last night!" Inquiries, of course, followed and the entire faculty began serious prayers for Mary Elaine and our family. Although I really did not understand all that was going on, I did have a sense of appreciation for the concern and intercession. I also had the feeling that Sister Carlice had sensed something when I had taken the note to her. It would have been typical of her to conceal her concern and to approach me in a casual manner that would not upset me.

Just before Lent each year, the school sponsored a Mardi Gras carnival. In every classroom a boy and girl were selected to be Mardi Gras prince or princess. On the night of the carnival, the royalty would process in and each person's name would be announced. Either because of my beautiful long hair, or because I was well liked at that age, I was selected from Miss Skelton's class. The boys were all to wear suits and the girls were to wear long dresses. I had been a flower girl at a wedding during the summer so I had an exquisite blue dress to wear. I could not have been more excited.

My moment of glory, however, was not to be. A day or so before the big night I got sick enough that I was not well in time for the carnival. I was crushed, but I had a sense of humor about the whole thing. One of my friends who had been to the carnival called me laughing and told me that when he got to my class, the announcer named the boy and then said, ". . . accompanying Beverly Pangle, who is ill this evening." We had never heard ourselves referred to as "ill" and we thought it was hysterically funny for me to have been announced that way.

EARLY IN THE SPRING of that year something wonderful happened. One day, just before we went to lunch, Miss Skelton took a special chalk holder that was designed to draw lines for musical notation. It held five pieces of chalk. Miss Skelton alternated the chalk, beginning with blue, then red, and so on. She then used this tool to make one long set of five lines on the board. We asked her what that was for, and she told us it was for a very special surprise that we would find out about after recess.

All during lunch and recess, my friends and I talked about what the surprise could be. When we got settled at the end of recess, Miss Skelton went to the board and with a piece of blue chalk, she carefully printed the word "ball" in lower-case letters. Slowly it sunk in that the lines on the board looked like our primary school paper. She had written the letters so that they fit on the lines correctly in the way we had been taught. Suddenly, we knew what was going on. "We're going to learn cursive writing!" several students squealed.

Miss Skelton confirmed this and thus began our first lesson. She took a piece of red chalk and went over the printed word to show us how the letters would change in cursive writing. Then she actually wrote "ball" in cursive right next to this demonstration. We were enthralled. She passed out some of the primary paper and we practiced for a while. Then she told us it was time to do some arithmetic. The protests were loud and plaintive. We wanted to learn more of this wonderful new method, but she did not relent. She told us that it was much more important for us to take it slowly and learn to write correctly. Reluctantly, we moved to math.

On subsequent days we would receive our Palmer Method writing books, and we would practice and practice our "O's" that were connected and which resembled sprung slinkies, and the up and down lines that looked like an unusual EKG reading. It still mystifies me that something as ordinary as learning cursive writing could have been introduced to us in such a thrilling way. I marvel at the level of teaching skill required.

The most important thing I remember about Easter that year is that I was seven. This meant that although I did not have to follow the same fasting rules as the adults, I was required to follow the rules of abstaining from meat. At that time, Catholics who were seven or older were forbidden to eat meat on Friday. During Lent, we also abstained on Ash Wednesday and Holy Saturday. Generally, I thought it was great to have this little way of outwardly demonstrating that I was Catholic. I always wanted meat on Friday, but the privilege of being Catholic and making this little sacrifice outweighed the temptation to eat it.

The exception was that Lent during second grade. Mom always fixed a ham for Easter dinner. She cooked it the night before, very slowly on a low setting, and would take it out of the oven just before she went to bed. I had not eaten meat on Friday or all day Saturday, and I was fine, until that night. All evening I could smell the wonderful aroma of the baking ham. Finally, I could stand it no more. I begged my mom to let me stay up until midnight so that I could have a taste of that delectable meat. I suppose to reward my adherence to the abstinence, she acquiesced.

I had no idea that this meant she had to stay up even beyond that in order for the Easter Bunny to make an appearance. The ham that night after midnight is probably the best-tasting ham I have ever had. I do not remember, but we must have forgotten about the after-midnight rule for fasting for Communion because I am certain I did go to Communion on Easter Sunday.

AS THE END of the school year and my eighth birthday approached, one of my aunts decided to give me her old bicycle. I was tickled to death. It was a twenty-six inch bike, old and plain, but in very good condition. The only problem was that I did not know how to ride it. For about two weeks, I constantly implored Mom to go outside with me so that I could practice riding. She would walk along beside me holding on to the back of the seat while I tried to get the feel of balancing the thing. We spent hours at this activity, but I remained afraid of her letting go.

One evening after supper, I begged her to go outside with me. She just did not have time. Daddy was busy doing some paperwork and my older brother was definitely not on the list of possibilities. I went back to my mother and pleaded one more time. This time she firmly told me that if I was that interested, I should just go get on the bike and ride it. She followed that sentence with a revelation. She had been letting go of the seat for the past few days when we had practiced and I could ride fine by myself. I was indignant. How could she have deceived me that way! She left me to wallow and within a few minutes I got up and determined that I would show everyone. I would ride that bike without any help. I can still vividly remember the sense of accomplishment when I went outside and did exactly that. Mom has always been a very wise woman.

When I got to school, I could not wait to tell my friends what I could do. Each afternoon I would hurry home, do my homework, and race outside to ride. Soon I was zooming everywhere, including down our steep driveway—sometimes with "no hands" or "no feet." I was very confident. Then it happened. I took a nasty fall. My pride was crushed, and my elbow looked disgusting. We only had about a week left of school, but I got miles of sympathy out of the bandaged arm, which I kept in a sling. It really was quite painful and as days passed, became increasingly inflamed around the abrasions.

Before it healed, I actually ran a fever and was sick from the whole accident. It served to put a blur on the end of second grade and my good-bye to my beloved Miss Skelton.

Chapter Three

"Sister Roche brought us around to the simple fact that prayer is talking to God and being quiet in order to hear His response."

WHEN I RECOVERED from my fall off the bike, I eagerly went back and tried again. That summer was definitely my "summer of freedom." I rode all over my neighborhood and felt very carefree. Although they were mostly younger than I was, there were always kids in the area to play with. I spent my days setting up lemonade stands, looking for evidence of fairies under the moss in the woods, and playing school.

As fall approached once more, I began praying. Sister Honoria was one of the students' favorite teachers and she taught third grade. I was dying to have her as my teacher. More important, I was terrified at the idea of having the other third-grade teacher, Sister Georgius. She had a very severe look about her and a reputation to match. I absolutely begged God to keep me out of her classroom because I knew I would not survive.

When the little postcards arrived, I got what I wanted. I was not to be in Sister Georgius' class. However, I was not in Sister Honoria's class either. To my horror, she had been transferred and I was assigned to Sister Roche's class. To make matters even worse, almost all of my friends were in the other room. Out of the fifteen or so girls in Sister Roche's class, I only knew three or four of them.

Since Sister Roche was new to the school, no one knew anything about her. I am not sure even now that I know much about her. She was very difficult to classify. She was old and sometimes seemed to border on senility, yet she was lively and could be feisty. Even with her occasional memory lapses, Sister Roche was an excellent teacher.

For some peculiar reason, there was a working telephone on the floor of our classroom. One of the first things that Sister Roche taught us was telephone etiquette. She drilled us on this frequently and when she was satisfied that we had mastered our telephone manners, she began letting us answer the phone on the rare occasions that it rang. She also took this opportunity to discuss what was and was not an acceptable lie. She wanted us to understand that there was such a thing as brutal honesty, which was inappropriate.

We began to realize that telling the exact truth takes discernment. Sister Roche took a very long time explaining all of this. We progressed to examples of whether we should tell someone they look awful simply because that is the truth, or whether we should spare their feelings. We even talked about the appropriateness of pointing out an imperfection. If, for example, as a girl headed out the door, her friend noticed her slip was showing, that friend should speak up so that the girl could make an adjustment before leaving the house. On the other hand, if that same girl was out in public with no possible way of fixing the situation, the friend should ignore the whole thing.

At the same time, Sister Roche emphasized the importance of telling the truth in the area of our own culpability in a given situation. As I look back, I cannot help but feel gratitude that Sister Roche spent an entire lesson on this chapter of politeness and the subtleties involved. I also realize sometimes how much some of our public figures could use a good dose of Sister Roche in their dealings with the public trust.

✎ DURING FIRST GRADE, our assignments came from worksheets, workbooks, and paperback texts. In second grade, we progressed to a hardback reader. Now in third grade, along with the reader, we had hardback English grammar books and arithmetic books. I was already familiar with the grammar book and the reader, but the English book had what I considered a most beautiful picture. It was in color and had two girls drawn with long dresses, one red and the other yellow. The unusual thing about the dresses is that they were made of leaves. I loved to look at that page in the book. It always gave me such a cozy, fall feeling. To this day, whenever I see beautiful red and yellow fall foliage together, I think of my third grade grammar book.

I also enjoyed the reader, or rather readers, that year. We had two, and both had red covers. Denise, one of my many cousins, had already read some of the stories from these books to me. When I arrived at school that year, I could hardly wait to read them again myself. One story that I particularly liked was about two girls who show up at the wrong house for a Halloween costume party. They both went dressed as pumpkins. At least that's what I think the story was about. The only thing I clearly remember was the picture of the two girls in their costumes.

Using a textbook for arithmetic really made us feel grown up. Second grade had just been a review of addition and subtraction with a few exercises in thought problems. In third grade, Sister Roche told us we would learn to multiply and divide. This was both exciting and scary to me. Although I would work ahead in most of my other subjects, I never did that in math. It was just too intimidating.

In religion, we learned the "Apostles Creed," and we began to prepare for the sacrament of Confirmation. Although this sacrament is now administered in the early teen years, during that time, it was done the year after First Communion. I remember very clearly Sister Roche talking to us about the meaning of prayer. After many students offered their opinions, she brought us around to the simple fact that prayer is talking to God and being quiet in order to hear his response. It was Sister Roche who first used the term "mental prayer" with us. This was when it began to dawn on me that there was more to praying than just repeating memorized prayers. We learned that formal prayers were only tools to get us started.

During the first part of the school year, the church was being remodeled and Masses were held in the gym. At some point, the fasting rules were changed and this made it easier to receive Communion. We could eat solid food up to three hours before reception, and liquids could be taken up to one hour before. In order to ensure that students could eat breakfast before coming to school, Mass time was moved from eight o'clock in the morning to eleven. I found all these changes very exciting.

Another thing that changed during that year was our visits to the school library. It really was not much to see. Located in a small room next to the school office, the library consisted of several bookshelves, which were sparsely adorned with books. In second grade, we had made one trip across the hall to this room in order to acquaint ourselves with library procedures. At that visit I had checked out a Little Golden Book with a Halloween story about a witch named Hazel. That was all it took to get me hooked on reading for pleasure.

When Sister Roche took us to the library the next year, I carefully picked out my book from the meager selection. It had a green cover and it was a real, hard-backed book. Not surprisingly, the subject matter was religious. It was about a little girl who had died young and who would become Saint Imelda. As it happened, I went home sick that afternoon, and spent the next few days reading my wonderful book while recuperating.

Again, the magazine sale rolled around, and my brother reminded me of our previous agreement. I pored over the catalogue of prizes and this time saw something incredibly special. My brother told me that if I wanted that prize, I would have to help sell some magazines. This posed absolutely no problem because I definitely had to have that item. We worked hard and by the deadline he not only had enough points for all the prizes he wanted, but I could get my dazzling trinket too. It was a beautiful, pearl bracelet. Dangling from the bracelet was a little silver box that looked like a prayer-book. The front and back of the box had imitation mother-of-pearl on it, and there was a silver cross on top of the mother-of-pearl on the front. Best of all, the prayer-book box opened and inside was a lovely, tiny rosary with pale green crystal beads. It was truly the most exquisite thing I had ever seen.

The rosary and mother-of-pearl prayer-book box Beverly received for selling magazines in third grade.

When I got the prize bracelet, I began saying one rosary after another. One day, I went to school and proudly told Sister Roche that I had said seven rosaries the night before. I do not remember her exact words, but I do remember how patiently she talked to me about this. First, she wanted to know why I said so many rosaries. I showed her the bracelet and explained how much I loved it. She must have caught on that in my gratitude for receiving this treasure, I had felt an exaggerated need to be thankful. She reined me in on this, and explained in a very kind way about quality of prayer versus quantity. I left her that day feeling very good about myself, yet also with a valuable lesson on true spirituality.

✎ THE TWO THIRD-GRADE classrooms were upstairs in the school building. One day, after being in school for a few weeks, we came back from Mass in our usual lines. For some reason as we made our way into the building and up the stairs, we had to stop for several minutes right on the stairway. The boys were on one side of the steps and the girls were on the other. We were to keep absolute silence at times like this, and while we were waiting for the lines to move, Sister Georgius made her way up the middle of the stairs. She was intending to keep order, but I did not see her. Before I knew it, she was right behind me and she put her hand on my shoulder in order to steady herself. There must have been a build-up of static electricity because when she touched me, she shocked me. I was instantly convinced that she was evil, and that electricity shot out of her fingers.

I could not wait to get outside after lunch and tell my old friends who were now in her class. As I told my little story, I was astounded to learn that my friends were mildly shocked that I would have such an opinion of their dear Sister Georgius. They informed me that they were glad they had gotten her for a teacher and that sometimes she was even fun. This was the second time in my short school life that I had had to confront my own prejudices about someone. I felt like a louse.

Besides the fact that we had a telephone in our classroom, there was one other unique feature. We sometimes listened to the radio. This would happen in the afternoon. We always listened to the same program and it probably came on only once a week; or maybe Sister would only allow us to listen to it that often. I do not remember a thing about the program's content, but I do remember the theme song. It was "The Clock Song." I have often wondered if the program was something we were interested in or if it was something Sister Roche particularly enjoyed. Either way we felt grateful for the reprieve from our classwork.

Physical education class had been practically nonexistent for the first two years of school. I do not have any clear memory of having PE in first grade. In second grade, on an occasional basis, a nice man named Coach Fleming would take the entire class outside for some type of exercise. It usually consisted of calisthenics of some sort and relays. Although Mr. Fleming was a very nice man, I missed my regular teacher and I did not like PE. (Almost fifteen years later, during my senior year in college, I would run into Mr. Fleming again. I was all the way across the state in Memphis doing my student teaching. When I arrived at my assigned school on the first day, I was directed to see the assistant principal, Mr. Fleming. It was such a good feeling, after all those years had passed, to see him again. I had been very apprehensive about the student teaching experience, and this certainly allayed my fears.)

In third grade, we had PE once a week with Coach Pfeifer. He seemed like a giant to me, and he was stern, in a fatherly sort of way. We did the usual relays and exercises, and, as always, I hated it. I was much too shy to compete on a relay team. I did not want to let anyone down, and I hated having the focus on me while I was doing my part of the race. It was not long before I came up with a plan. Sister Roche seemed to like me, and she would occasionally allow me to grade papers for her. Somehow, I convinced her one day to let me stay out of gym class to do this.

One of my classmates, who also hated PE, noticed I was not there and asked me where I had been. Not realizing her distress with the activity, I eagerly told her what Sister Roche had let me do. A couple of weeks later, I decided to try the same trick again. This time, my classmate, who had made certain to keep an eye on me, volunteered herself too. Surprisingly, Sister Roche said yes to both of us, and we smugly watched the others line up for gym. She and I began grading papers, and Sister Roche left the room for a few minutes to take the others down the stairs to Coach Pfeifer and to stop off at the office.

My accomplice and I were engrossed in our activity a few minutes later when we heard a booming male voice say, "What are you girls doing in here?" It was Coach Pfeifer and he looked serious. Meekly, I told him we were grading papers for Sister Roche. Very firmly he informed us that he was sure she did not intend for us to make a habit of missing PE in order to grade papers, and he told us to quickly get outside with the rest of our class. When we hesitated, since Sister Roche was not in the room at the time, he told us he would take care of speaking to her about it. He added that we should never pull a stunt like that again. Humiliated, we went to PE, and I never tried such a thing again. Sister Roche never mentioned a word to either of us. This always made me a little suspicious that it had all been a set-up to make an impression on us. In my case, it certainly worked.

THERE WERE SEVERAL opportunities in third grade to demonstrate charity toward our fellow classmates. Two little girls had not yet made it to school that year. Sister carefully explained to us that we must pray for these two because they were seriously ill. Betty was one of the girls, and I believe she had rheumatic fever. The other child was named Ann. I do not really remember what she had, but it caused her to lose most of her hair. We prayed for these girls daily, and we eagerly awaited any progress reports about them. When they were allowed to come back to school, we felt that our prayers had helped.

Sister also carefully prepared us for their return. We were told that Betty had to be very careful about physical activity. We watched over her like mother hens, squawking at her if she even thought about running on the playground. We had been cautioned that she could suffer a relapse or worse, and we were not about to let that happen.

Although Ann had lost most of her hair, and we had been warned of this, by the time she came back to school, it did not seem that awful to us. I do not mean that we did not sympathize with her. Rather, we were immediately very accepting of her and simply not shocked by her appearance.

Whether because of the illnesses of these two girls or because of some unknown reason, I decided to play a trick on two of my friends, Maggi and Mary Catherine. One day, at recess, I became very somber. They insisted on knowing what was wrong, and after sufficient begging, I confided to them that in fact I was dying. My intention had been to immediately laugh and tell them I was teasing, but I did not get the chance. They were grief-stricken. They hovered around me and were all but in tears. I was torn between enjoyment of the out-pouring of sympathy and my own guilt. Thank goodness, my guilt won out. They were quite stunned at my admission of the joke.

Their disappointment made a huge impression on me. I understood that I had put them in the position of displaying their raw emotions for the sake of "fun." I knew it was a huge betrayal, and I immediately made every attempt to resolve things with a sincere heart. They were both such good, conscientious girls that they did not make me endure their disappointment very long. For my part, I promised never to do anything so deceitful again.

There were two other opportunities to demonstrate compassion that year. The first involved a guy named Richie who had been in my class since first grade. One day for some inexplicable reason, Richie decided to stand on the wide railing atop the open stairwell on the second floor. Unfortunately, he fell. Miraculously, he survived, but he was severely injured. Our little prayers stormed heaven, and after a very long time, he did return to school.

The focus in the examples of the two sick girls and the injured boy was always on them. Today, when tragic things happen, school officials often seem to worry to the extreme about the effects of such news on the healthy students. While I certainly agree that school personnel need to be vigilant regarding the state of mind of each student, I sometimes feel that this is blown out of proportion. When something unfortunate happens, the attention should first be on those directly affected by the tragedy. Students should be led to empathize with the person and family members involved. Too often, the emphasis turns toward how this news affects the one hearing it. I sometimes wonder if this is not partially due to the discomfort of the adults who are in charge. Whatever the reasons, I feel we do our youth a disservice by not encouraging them to exhibit strength and compassion.

Our final major call to kindness that year came with a circumstance none of us had yet encountered. One day a young girl in braids appeared at the door to our classroom. Some adults and an older boy accompanied her with Sister St. Camillus, our principal. As the adults spoke to Sister Roche, the girl timidly looked around. Within a few minutes, this little group left the classroom and Sister closed the door. Very quietly, she explained to us that the little girl and her family had escaped from Hungary and made their way to the United States. They would be living in Chattanooga for a while, and the little girl would be our new classmate. We were to be very patient with her because although she could speak English, she needed time to process what we said when we spoke to her.

Sister Roche went on to tell us how fortunate we were to live in a country with religious freedom. She told us that the refugee family had endured many hardships just to be able to enjoy what we so often took for granted. By the time Sister finished talking to us, we could not wait for the little girl to come back to class. Her story fascinated us. We had heard stories about courageous people struggling to practice their faith, but now we would have someone right in our midst. We felt honored that the new family had come to our city.

The little girl's name was Kathleen. She had dark, blonde hair that she often wore in braids, and she had a ruddy complexion. She was initially shy, but quickly warmed up to us. The best thing about her from my point of view was that she rode my bus in the afternoon. We sat together each day and chattered until we reached her house. It was about halfway to my house and it sat high on a hill. I had always noticed this particular house because not only did it seem large to me, it also seemed lonely and in need of paint. I was glad that a nice family like Kathleen's had moved into it. I just knew they would appreciate the old house.

THIRD GRADE brought me my first real admirer. His name was John Davis. He was a cute boy with light brown hair that was streaked blonde from the summer sun. John absolutely doted on me. He lived near the school at that time, and at the end of the day while I was waiting for the bus, he would ride his bike in circles around me. Unfortunately, his devotion was unrequited. Since second grade I had had a huge crush on three boys who were brothers. I would not give John the time of day. I was not mean, but I was not encouraging either.

Occasionally, I would get annoyed with John for pestering me during class. One time he snatched my autograph book and wrote "I love you" on one of the pages. This outpouring of emotion panicked me and I complained to Sister Roche. Although she got after him, it was in such a way that made me think I should appreciate the attention rather than whine about it. He did stop bothering me during class, but I was the one who felt guilty.

As the year progressed, someone noticed a picture of a young girl that hung in the classroom. Sister told us it was Saint Maria Goretti, who was a martyr. It seems that at twelve years old Maria was already very pretty. A teenage boy who lived on her parents' property was attracted to her and kept making unwanted advances. One day, when he cornered her alone in her house and she again refused him, he stabbed and killed her. The boy was sentenced to life in prison and as an old man was still living when Sister told us the story. I often looked at the beautiful picture and thought about Maria Goretti's courage. Although I was too young to be battling with purity issues, I wanted to emulate her commitment. When we prepared for Confirmation and were instructed to select the name of a saint for our Confirmation name, my choice was easy. Of course, my name would be Maria.

As time for Confirmation drew near, we earnestly studied our *Baltimore Catechism.* Sister Roche told us exactly what to expect, and most of us focused our attention on the "slap" on the cheek that the bishop would give to each of us. It was not unusual when we were on the playground to hear the bravado of one of the students who said, "Well, when the bishop hits me, I'm gonna hit him right back!" We all knew it was nervous humor, but what really caused us stress was the fact that during the ceremony we knew the bishop would orally quiz us on the knowledge of our faith. I do not know what terrified me most: failing in front of my parents, disappointing Sister Roche, or humiliating myself in front of my classmates.

Beverly's third-grade catechism.

The night of the ceremony finally came. The girls were required to wear white dresses, which meant that I would wear my First Communion dress. That was quite all right with me except for one thing. I had grown quite a bit in the year since I had worn it last, and we did not consider that until it was too late. My dress was a wee bit short, but thank goodness, it did not cause me to feel embarrassed. On our heads, we wore these ridiculous red beanies with three, short red tabs sticking up on top. I know the girls especially must have looked comical with the little yarmulke-like caps perched precariously on their bouncy curls. All of us had to secure the hats with bobby pins.

At my mother's suggestion, I had chosen one of my dad's cousins as my sponsor. This adult was supposed to accept the responsibility of being an example and guiding me in my faith. Barbara Laub was a wonderful choice. Although we never really had a conversation about the Catholic faith, she was an excellent model of someone living her faith. She gave me two gifts for the occasion. One was a beautiful holy card depicting Mary as the Immaculate Conception. The other was a silver ring with a blue Immaculate Conception medal.

Our class met that evening in our classroom and processed over to the church. It was December and I remember that it was cold walking outside without our coats. We had rehearsed all week and everything went smoothly. No one missed a question, and I do not believe I had to answer any at all. The big "slap" was a mere tap, but there were some wise guys who walked away rubbing their cheeks. When we were dismissed after the ceremony, my family, Barbara, and her daughter came to our house for a small celebration.

The holy card that Barbara gave me for Confirmation began an obsession for me. In fact, all the girls in my class were fascinated with holy cards. We began trading them the way the boys traded baseball cards. However, we were much worse. We did our trading during Mass! I do not know how otherwise conscientious children managed to be so rude, but somehow we rationalized our behavior. After all, we must have thought, these were "holy" cards. Surely, God would not mind if we exchanged them with each other. Well, maybe God did not, but the teachers did. By the time Sister Roche realized what we were doing, we had become hopelessly hooked. She lectured us often, and kept her eye out for those who paid her no heed, but it did not stop us. We just became very furtive in our activity, and only slightly curtailed it. In time, I acquired quite a collection.

EVERY YEAR, two or three months before Christmas, Daddy would bring home a huge catalogue. The Hahn Company produced it, and I suppose it resembled a Spiegel catalog. My brothers and I would peruse the toy section and find many toys and gadgets that we had not seen anywhere else. We would tell Mom about the things we wished for, and, of course, on Christmas morning we were never disappointed.

For whatever reason, I do not remember seeing that catalog the year that I was in third grade, but Christmas morning brought squeals of delight anyway. One of my most prized gifts from Santa was what my mom always referred to as my "teenage doll." This was a year before Barbie would appear on the scene, and this doll was exquisite. She had long, brunette hair that could be styled, and blue eyes that opened and closed. Her arms and legs moved in two places each, and her head could move on her neck and she could be twisted at the waist. The most remarkable thing was her wardrobe. It was beautiful! It came with every imaginable change of outfit, plus undergarments! I don't know if Mom ordered it from the catalog, but I know it was the most wonderful doll I ever owned.

When we got back to school after the holidays, Sister Roche told us that we could bring one of our favorite things that we had received for Christmas and show the class. Of course, I took my doll. Each of us took our item up to Sister's desk, one at a time. She then let us take our time showing it to the class and talking about it. For those who were timid, she helped with the commentary. When it came to my turn, I took everything, doll and wardrobe up to her desk. Sister was enthralled with my doll. She had me show the class each of the outfits in the little wardrobe case, and she could not get over the tiny high-heeled shoes.

When everything had been examined, I collected all of the pieces and hurried back to my seat. Sister chuckled and said, “Beverly, I think you forgot something.” As I looked up, I was mortified to see her holding up the doll’s bra! Embarrassed, I took the undergarment out of her hand while my friends shook with laughter. By the time I got back to my seat, I thought it was funny too; the site of a nun dangling a miniature bra from her fingers was comical.

In January or February of that school year, we had a huge snowfall. We woke up to it on a Saturday. The city was paralyzed. The kids in my neighborhood were astounded because we were not used to snow. Daddy and the next-door neighbor decided to go out and buy a sled. They found a large one that would hold four or five adults, and because it was expensive, they went in together on the purchase. That weekend was glorious. We made a wonderful snowman with my dad. We drank gallons of hot chocolate—the real thing—none of the instant stuff we have now. Most of all, though, we rode the sled or the dishpans down the many hills around our house.

The weekend was so much fun that I did not want it to end. When Mom woke me up for school on Monday morning, I could not bear to go. I told her I was not feeling well. I really whined, and surprisingly very quickly, she said I could stay home. I should have known I was about to learn a lesson. About ten minutes after Mom told me I could stay in bed, my older brother let out a big whoop. He had just heard on the radio that the Catholic schools were closed. In fact, all the schools in the city were closed. This was great, I thought, as I jumped out of bed to quickly dress for outdoor fun. When I went into the kitchen, Mom burst my bubble immediately. She told me that if I had been too sick to get up for school, I was too sick to go outside.

Soon everyone else in my family and most of the neighborhood kids were in our yard having the time of their lives. Mom even invited friends from across the city to drive over for sledding since they had chains on their cars and could maneuver on the icy streets. I was miserable. This was one time that Mom really held her ground with me. She only briefly relented and let me go out for thirty minutes, but she kept track of the time, and I did not stay out a second longer. Luckily for me, the schools were closed for the week, but my punishment only lasted that one day.

ALTHOUGH I LOVED spiritual hymns, I was also very patriotic. One day, Sister Roche told the class that we were going to learn a beautiful song about our country. We spent much of the afternoon copying the words as she dictated them, and then we practiced the song. I thought it was a wonderful song and could not wait to get home and tell my mom what I had learned. I jumped off the school bus and ran flying into the kitchen to greet Mom. Breathlessly, I told her we had learned a special song. She eagerly asked me what it was, and when I told her, she laughed uproariously. As she composed herself, she giggled and told me she looked forward to Daddy's return from work so that I could tell him about the song. By this time, I was confused, and told her I did not see what was so funny. Finally, she said,

"Honey, it's not 'My Country 'Tis a Flea;' it's 'My Country 'Tis of Thee.' " That confused me even more because I really thought the words were, "My country 'tis aflee . . ." meaning that the people in the country during the Revolutionary War had been fleeing or something. Needless to say, the beauty of that song was lost on me for a while; at least until the laughter of my family subsided.

As spring came that year, Charlie, one of the boys in our class, brought wonderful news. His family had a farm and they had an abundance of baby chicks. On a certain day, his parents would bring the chicks to school and at dismissal they would distribute the cute little things to those who had permission to take them. Reluctantly, Mom acquiesced to my request. The day arrived and we each received our chick in a box that resembled a Chinese restaurant take-out box with holes in it. I carefully took my instantly beloved treasure onto the school bus.

When I arrived home, I took it out of the box to show Mother. The poor little animal was shaking and terrified. Thinking it was cold, I somehow convinced Mom to put it in the oven with the door open. She had the temperature setting on warm. Who would have thought that that would slow-cook the creature? When it slowly closed its little eyes, I just thought it was finally warm, and peacefully dropping off to sleep. I was horrified in the next instant to realize that it was dead.

I insisted on a funeral. Mom found an old canning jar, and we placed the little chick inside. Reverently, we went to the woods behind the house, and buried the short-lived pet. I was crushed, and felt like a murderer. Most of those baby chickens that were handed out met similar fates. If they served any purpose in their brief lives, it was to demonstrate how fragile and precious life is.

I was not the only student who missed many days of school each year. A boy named Donald also missed quite a few. Sister Roche thought the two of us could do better, and when I had accumulated about fourteen absences, she called me to her desk. Rather sternly she told me that a person could be held back a grade if he or she missed more than thirty days of school a year. Since the year still had a long way to go, she wanted me to keep that in mind when I felt I needed to stay home. She told the same thing to the boy.

At first, I felt humiliated and I was determined not to miss. Then my many little illnesses pursued me and, together with my desire to be home with Mother, caused me to give in and stay home. I was meticulous about making up my work and eventually I earned Sister's respect on that score. However, I was constantly aware of not going over the thirty-day figure. By the end of the year, I had missed somewhere around twenty-six or twenty-eight days.

Sister Roche was fiercely loyal to her students. An incident near the end of the school year exemplified this trait. We third-grade girls felt that the fourth-grade girls were rather snobby. We usually just left them to themselves. As the school year drew to a close, they began to delight in picking on us during recess. This mostly consisted of mild insults, but because they were unprovoked, we were quite indignant.

Finally, a group of us complained to Sister. She went scurrying over to the fourth-grade teacher's room and very firmly insisted that the teacher put an immediate stop to the inappropriate behavior. Poor Sister Lena, who was such a dear, was mortified. She assured Sister Roche that she would take care of it, and she did. The remainder of the school year was uneventful, and I looked forward to a relaxing and fun-filled summer vacation.

Chapter Four

"Mom casually mentioned to me that several of my friends had made the first honor roll, and both she and Sister Lena thought I could do that too. Needless to say, that was all it took."

SISTER LENA had been my older brother's fourth-grade teacher, and I had hoped all summer that she would be mine too. When my postcard arrived, I was delighted to find that my dream had come true. On the first day of school, as we assembled in the classroom, we received a shock. Sister Lena would only be teaching the girls! The boys were in a classroom across the hall. I think most of us were actually happy about this, that is, until we got a glimpse of the other fourth-grade teacher. From a distance, for a few jealous moments, we thought that our beloved first-grade teacher, Sister Carlice, had returned to teach them. The new nun across the hall was beautiful and she was young, but she was not Sister Carlice. Her name was Sister Leonine.

I really don't think we were told why we were separated by gender that year. It had never happened before, and did not happen again to any class. Whatever the reason, I was thrilled. I was becoming increasingly shy, and I felt much more comfortable without the boys. For her part, Sister Lena was a dear. She was holiness personified. I do not remember her ever raising her voice, although she did have to correct us from time to time. She was loving and incredibly gentle, but she urged us to pursue excellence. She was a thorough teacher with a knack for explaining things.

The previous year, I had noticed that most of the fourth-grade girls pushed the sleeves of their sweaters up to their elbows. For some inexplicable reason, I had decided that this looked quite grown-up. I was ready to follow their example, and I looked forward to cool, fall mornings when I could do just that. This marked the point in my life when I realized I really was not a baby anymore.

We added another subject to our curriculum in fourth grade: geography. I absolutely loved reading in this book. We followed the travels of a boy named Peter as he went around the world with his father. Although I thoroughly enjoyed the stories and learned a lot from the textbook, it was not easy. At times, I found the questions that we had for homework quite challenging. This made it my most difficult subject and cemented in my mind that fourth grade was the first step to maturity.

PUNCTUATING this theme was the fact that, for the first time in our lives, six weeks' grades were used to determine honor rolls. First honor roll required having more "A's" than "B's" and nothing lower. Second honor roll required any combination of "B's" or "A's" in which the "B's" dominated and with nothing lower. For my first six weeks, I made the second honor roll. Parent/teacher conferences were held at that time, and Mom and Dad returned home with a glowing report about me from Sister Lena. Mom did casually mention to me that she noticed several of my friends had made the first honor roll, and that both she and Sister Lena thought I could do that too. Needless to say, that was all it took. The rest of the year I was determined to accomplish this, and felt very proud of myself when I succeeded.

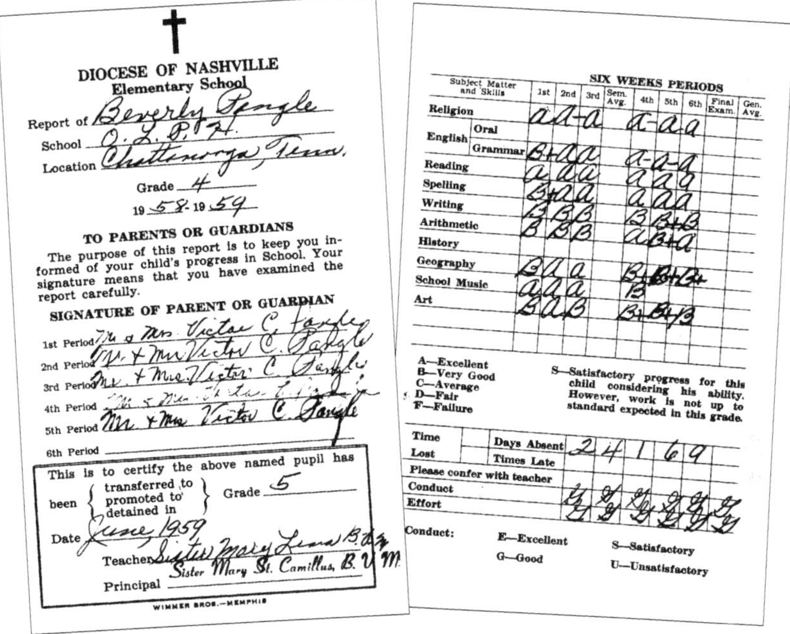

DIOCESE OF NASHVILLE
Elementary School

Report of Beverly Pangle
School O.L.P.H.
Location Chattanooga, Tenn.
Grade 4
19 58 - 19 59

TO PARENTS OR GUARDIANS

The purpose of this report is to keep you informed of your child's progress in School. Your signature means that you have examined the report carefully.

SIGNATURE OF PARENT OR GUARDIAN

1st Period Mr & Mrs. Victor C. Pangle
2nd Period Mr. + Mrs Victor C. Pangle
3rd Period Mr. + Mrs. Victor C. Pangle
4th Period Mr. + Mrs. Victor C. Pangle
5th Period Mr. + Mrs Victor C. Pangle
6th Period

This is to certify the above named pupil has been transferred to / promoted to / detained in Grade 5

Date June, 1959
Teacher Sister Mary Lena B.V.M.
Principal Sister Mary St. Camillus, B.V.M.

WIMMER BROS.—MEMPHIS

Subject Matter and Skills		1st	2nd	3rd	Sem. Avg.	4th	5th	6th	Final Exam.	Gen. Avg.
Religion		A	A-	A		A-	A	A		
English	Oral									
	Grammar	B+	A	A		A-	A-	A		
Reading		A	A	A		A	A	A		
Spelling		B+	A	A		A	A	A		
Writing		B	B	B		B	B+	B		
Arithmetic		B	B	B		A	B+	A		
History										
Geography		B	A	A		B+	B+	A+		
School Music		A	A	A		B				
Art		B	A	B		B+	B+	B		

A—Excellent
B—Very Good
C—Average
D—Fair
F—Failure

S—Satisfactory progress for this child considering his ability. However, work is not up to standard expected in this grade.

Time Lost							
Days Absent	2	4	1	6	9		
Times Late							
Please confer with teacher							
Conduct	G	G	G	G	G	G	
Effort	G	G	G	G	G	G	

Conduct: E—Excellent G—Good S—Satisfactory U—Unsatisfactory

Beverly's fourth-grade report card.

Another way I noticed that we were demonstrating our maturity was by our abandonment of the exaggerated sing/song unison speaking. Beginning with our first days in first grade, we had been taught how to reply correctly as a group when someone in authority spoke to us. We began rather timidly at this endeavor, but quickly progressed to the more comical inflections for our "Yes, Sister" or "Thank you, Sister," etc. We realized how cute we sounded and were eager to get a reaction from any visitor to our classrooms. By fourth grade, the novelty had worn off, and we felt babyish answering in that manner. Thus, our replies took on a genuinely polite tone.

One of the prayers that we learned in fourth grade was the "Angelus." The church had a carillon and each day at noon the bells for the "Angelus" rang. After learning the prayer, it was not unusual to see us stop our playing on the blacktop and reverently recite this prayer upon hearing the bells. Most of us probably did this more to please Sister Lena than because of piety. We dearly loved her, and wanted her to know that we paid attention to what she taught us.

Although it might have happened before fourth grade, this is the year I remember our periodic visits to the church, when Father Bush would quiz us on our progress in the catechism. I was terrified of these occasions, and I don't understand why. My knees literally knocked together during these sessions. Father Bush was an old-fashioned priest who could be stern, but who had a wonderful sense of humor. He definitely expected us to know our catechism, but I don't ever remember him raising his voice during these meetings. Whenever he asked a question, I repeated the answer over and over in my mind before raising my hand. Occasionally, he would just call on someone and then ask the question. This is what I feared most.

I can honestly say that I don't ever remember giving an incorrect answer during the years that Father Bush met with us like this, but my terror never lessened. Sometimes, a student would miss a question. When this happened with one of Sister Lena's students, I remember how disappointed she would be. Her disappointment seemed to go deeper than embarrassment over the fact that one of her students had seemed ill prepared. I felt she took the responsibility of our religious instruction so seriously that she could not bear to think she had failed to get essential points across. To me, her distress was a reflection of her abiding love for us rather than relative to her ego.

The practice of memorizing the answers to the questions from the *Baltimore Catechism* would be severely criticized as I got older. I have never agreed with this negative assessment. When a mother bird wants to nourish her young, she ingests the food first and then regurgitates it into the mouths of the little creatures. The Church is our mother and when we are young we need the benefit of her wisdom to supply us with our spiritual nourishment. The fact that the *Baltimore Catechism* provided this in a predigested form was well suited to our capacity.

DURING THE FALL of that year, my Mom had a miscarriage. She had been about four months pregnant when it happened. I remember being more concerned about the fact that I had not even been told she was pregnant than I was about the loss to her and our family. She was in the hospital for a couple of days because of the miscarriage, and I missed her terribly. The day she got out, Daddy got off work early and brought her to school at the end of the day. As I walked out of the school building and down the steps, I spotted her and Daddy standing under a tree. I had not expected her, and a look of sheer joy spread over my face. Mom had been watching for me and later she told me how much it had meant to her that her homecoming was so exciting to me. As she fixed dinner for us that evening, I asked her about the lost baby. She almost cried as she talked, and this nearly broke my heart. I could not bear to see my mother sad. She must have sensed my distress, and she quickly composed herself.

Although sometimes people would tell Mom that she was high-strung and worried too much, I did not see that in her. She has always been fun-loving and ready for mischief. She broke her instep twice within the two years between my eighth and tenth birthdays. It happened the first time when she kicked a football out in our front yard. On the second occasion, she had just finished riding my brother's twenty-six-inch bicycle. She was stopped and had her feet on the ground, but because it was a boy's bike, it had the high bar across it. She was straddling this bar and her legs were just long enough for her feet to touch the ground. Suddenly, she lost her balance, the heavy front wheel turned and she fell over. The result was the broken foot.

These incidents are worth repeating because they illustrate that Mom enjoyed life and did not allow worry to consume her. During the football season when I was in fourth grade, I saw the other side of her. My older brother Clayton was in the eighth grade and played football. One afternoon, Mom was home with the rest of us, but Daddy took off work early to see Clayton's game. As it got later and she expected them home, the phone rang. It was Daddy, and he and Clayton were at the emergency room. It seems Clayton had broken his arm during the game.

When she got off the telephone, Mom began sobbing. Concerned, I asked her what was wrong. She filled me in on the details, and I tried to comfort her by pointing out that other than his arm being in a cast for a few weeks, Clayton was fine. It was the first time I realized how much she really worried about us. The nuns had always reinforced the idea that our parents loved and cared for us in a way that we were too young to understand, but which we should appreciate. On this day, the lesson sank in for me.

One of the students in my class was a beautiful girl named Elaine. She had dark brown hair, brown eyes, and a lovely olive complexion. Elaine had a very lively personality, but she was shy in the classroom. This was because she stuttered. I remember how lovingly and patiently Sister Lena would work with Elaine. She always encouraged her to read and answer orally in class. We took Elaine under our wings and gave her our support. On the playground, we praised her as she chattered with us and urged her to realize that she was just as safe with us in the classroom. She began to show real progress, but then her family had to move to another city and we all lost contact with her. I have often thought about Elaine, and wondered if her memories of us are as positive as my memory of her. I know that Sister Lena was sincere in her attempt to help Elaine and in teaching us a bit about compassion.

In fourth grade, I still rode the school bus home. My brother was in eighth grade and because he was such a responsible sort, he was appointed bus monitor. He ruled with an iron fist, standing up in front in the step-well. It was his duty to pull the door opener to let students off the bus. He also made certain everyone stayed in their seat, and that no one played with the emergency exit in the back of the bus.

The ride was long and noisy. I often arrived home with a terrible headache. My only consolation was that the three brothers I had a crush on also rode the bus. I only remember a few of the other regular riders. One was a boy named Donald. He was in fifth grade and always sat with a girl named Barbara. This was significant because Barbara was a little overweight, walked with a limp, and her hand on one side was permanently bent downward. Many of the students ignored Barbara. A few made fun of her. I talked to her a little, but because I was shy and she was older, not that often.

Donald, on the other hand, seemed like a true friend. I did not know him other than through that observation, but I always remembered his kindness to her. Ironically, he would enter my life years later as a childhood friend of my non-Catholic husband. Not only was Donald in our wedding, but he was the godfather of our elder daughter at her Baptism. While I was happy to have one of my husband's friends assume this responsibility, I was also comforted by my own memory of this man's kind heart.

At daily Mass during fourth grade there was still some holy card trading going on, but my attention was elsewhere. One of our prize possessions was our daily missal. I had a *Marian Missal.* My best friend had one that I liked better, a *Pius X Missal.* The *Marian Missal* had only one streamer to mark a place. The *Pius X Missal* had five colorful streamers. Best of all, the streamers were attached to a vinyl flap that tucked into the top of the binding and could be completely removed. We sometimes did this in order to braid the streamers. However, I was not completely devoid of piety during Mass. A few very lucky classmates had copies of books the size of our missals, but which contained the lives of the saints instead. If I were fortunate enough to talk one of these students into lending me her book, I would pore over the brief biographies of these saints and martyrs as Mass was progressing.

DURING this particular school year, I was confronted by the reality of death in three very different circumstances. The first came in October, 1958, with the death of Pope Pius XII. Sister Lena was very solemn as she told us this news, but she also told it with great hope. She carefully explained that the pope had been a very holy man with great faith, and that it was certain he was now enjoying the beatific vision. This was the only pope that there had been since my birth, and his death was both disconcerting and exciting for me.

At first, it was troubling because I did not understand what would happen to the Church without the pope. When Sister later explained the election process, I was enthralled. I misunderstood her explanation and thought the entire selection hinged on whether or not white smoke came out when the ballots were burned. This certainly heightened the mystery of the Church for me for a while. Of course, after a few chuckles from my older brother as I related the story at dinner, he set me straight.

The second encounter with death came with the news of a real tragedy. One morning in December, we noticed that faculty members, the nuns in particular, were very somber. They spoke to each other in subdued voices, and sometimes mournfully shook their heads. Finally, Sister Lena directed her attention to us. Quietly, she explained to us that the day before there had been a terrible fire in a Catholic school in Chicago. Over time, ninety students and three nuns would die as a result of this fire. These nuns were from the same order as our beloved BVMs, and the sadness in the school that day was palpable. We offered up many prayers for the victims and their families.

I could not easily forget the catastrophic fire and the probable devastation it had on the lives of the survivors and the families. One of my aunts subscribed to both *Look* and *Life* magazines and soon after the fire, we went to visit her on a Sunday afternoon. I remember poring over the article about the fire, which was in one of these magazines. I cringed at the panic that the children must have felt. I cried when I read about the frightened nun who had kept her students praying in the classroom awaiting rescue, only to perish with them. I knew she must have been terrified, bewildered, and left with no hope of survival. I kept replaying her decision and wishing she had done something else. I have never forgotten those children, many who were the same age as I was. Often I have looked with gratitude on my life and opportunities in light of the brevity of theirs.

My final exposure to death that school year came in February. One morning, a student named Ellen rushed into the classroom saying to all of us, "Did your hear? Did you hear? Buddy Holly, Richie Valens, and the Big Bopper were all killed in a plane crash!" This was monumentally shocking to me. I loved their music! I spent hours downstairs in our basement, skating to the beat of their songs. I loved to see the Big Bopper perform "Chantilly Lace" on the Ed Sullivan or American Bandstand shows. I could not imagine the world without them.

This was also the first time in my existence that a celebrity, not to mention three celebrities, had met a tragic death. I remember feeling a little lost for a while. The day I had heard the news, I went home from school and down to the basement put "La Bamba" on the stereo, and skated to it until suppertime. Down there, with nothing but the sound of the music and my skates, I made peace with the reality of death.

I AM STILL AMAZED when I realize how Sister Lena, as well as most of my other teachers, could make something very simple seem incredibly special. One of the ways that Sister Lena did this was through an extra set of readers, which were stacked in the back of the classroom. On certain days, she would heap praise on us for what we had accomplished that morning. We always knew what that meant. We would have some extra time before we would have to line up for the eleven o'clock Mass, and she would tell several students to pass out the special readers. I really don't know why we loved these books so, but we did. Not only did she increase our love of reading, but she also made us feel that we had earned a privilege by allowing us access to these books.

Sister Lena felt that a thorough review of what we had learned in our primary grades was very important. However, she was wise enough to realize that some of that review work might seem too babyish. She saw the value in phonics as an aid to spelling, but she knew that we felt much too grown-up for any direct approach. Instead, she made the phonics review fun. On those days when we had a few extra minutes before Mass, but not enough time to pass out the special books, she had us all stand next to our desks. We then ran down the sounds of the alphabet and spellings of various words that might give us trouble. This was all done with inflections that were rhythmic, which made the entire exercise something we enjoyed. Years later, when Dan Quayle committed his "potato" faux pas, I could not help but remember Sister Lena and her phonics drills. "Potato" was one of our words.

As the year passed, I began reading more and more books or pamphlets of a spiritual nature. My favorite topic was Our Lady of Fatima. No matter how many times I read about the three children who saw Our Lady, I was always moved to tears. I would say several rosaries each day and offer up as many little sacrifices as I could possibly think of to offer. Because the message talked about the many offenses committed against God, I was led to a new awareness of the passion of Our Lord. I read and reread the account of Christ's passion in our church history book. Although I remained cognizant of the events, it would be almost forty years before reflection on our Savior's gift would again stir the same sorrow in the depths of my soul.

Each day, after lunch and recess, Sister Lena would settle us down to an assignment and then select one student to accompany her. For some reason, she was in charge of a box of money that was apparently collected in the cafeteria. We did not have candy, but this money might have been from the sale of milk or ice cream. For whatever reason, Sister needed to take the box of money downstairs to the convent each day. Since she was a little feeble, it must have seemed wise to have a student go with her. We were always tickled to be selected as the designated companion. The trip was brief. We went down the hall, down two flights of stairs, and waited at the foot of the two steps that led to the interior door to the convent. Usually, our sole function would be to carry that box, which had once held Hersey bars. Sister would disappear into the convent for what seemed like only one or two minutes, and then we returned to class.

In the spring of that year, I have a very clear memory of a day that I was picked to go with Sister. We made the usual trek, but as she entered the convent, I noticed a warm breeze. Through the doorway, I could see the peaceful green walls of the convent and I noticed a green, chiffon curtain gently blowing in the breeze. I was transfixed. It was the only time in my life that I ever felt even the slightest pull toward a religious vocation. Because I have always felt certain that I am where I am supposed to be as a wife and mother, I look back on that day as a gift. I think I was given a brief glimpse of the peace that can exist within the religious life. Whatever the reason for the experience, it was one of those beautifully sublime moments that are so intensely personal any explanation or description is inadequate.

DURING MY GRADE-SCHOOL YEARS, we were required to take achievement tests on several occasions. The ones we took were called the Dayton Tests because they were developed, I believe, at the University of Dayton. I actually enjoyed taking them. I always looked upon standardized tests, with the bubble answer sheets, as game-like. Once it had been established that they had nothing to do with report card grades, I was up for the challenge. I particularly remember the administration of the tests in fourth grade. A team of examiners from the University of Dayton arrived at school to proctor the battery of tests. They were all women, as well as I can remember, and they were in uniform—either that or they just thought the way to look professional was to wear the same navy blue suit with matching heels. These were very stern-looking women.

When I saw them, I was reminded of matrons from old women's prison movies. We had been primed to treat these visitors with the utmost respect, and based on their looks, we did not need any coaxing. Although I was frightened of these monitors, I saw them as only a minor annoyance, except for one thing. I would throw myself into the task of doing my best on these tests. My focus was intense. When the time was up for a particular test segment, these women would say, "Stop! Put your pencils down!" Each time, it had the same jarring effect on me. I could not understand why they had to be so harsh in their approach.

It had such an effect on me that years later when I was an educator and would administer standardized tests, I would relate this story to my students before testing. I would promise them that I would gently alert them to the "time's up" cue. Looking back, I realize that those women had been trained to maintain the integrity of the tests, and that they were very conscientious. Their method was just a sharp contrast to our gentler teachers.

✎ AS THE YEAR drew to its close, I made the decision to go to Girl Scout Camp for a couple of weeks that summer. It was just a day camp, but there was swimming in a lake. This meant that a typhoid shot was required. I got my shot on the last day of school. We got out at noon that day, and I went straight to the doctor. That evening we would be back over at school for my brother's eighth-grade graduation and the awards ceremony that took place for grades four through eight. Of course, by the time evening approached, I was running a fever and my arm was red, swollen, and very sore.

The events of that night were too important to miss, so, miserable as I was, I went. I remember being in agony. My peers kept accidentally bumping into my arm, sending me into spasms of pain. The fever only made the pain seem worse. I was near tears the entire time, but I did not want anyone other than my family to know what was going on. Thus, I received my first pin ever for academic achievement, yet could not enjoy it. When I returned to my seat after receiving the little pin, I looked down and to my horror discovered a mistake. Instead of being inscribed "First Honors," it had "Perfect Attendance" engraved on it. Through my misery, I chuckled at the fact that I would now have an attendance pin in my possession. I knew that there was no chance that I would ever legitimately earn one.

Chapter Five

"Mrs. Fonseca was a very spiritual person. She was also very practical, and could have been described as having one foot in heaven and the other planted firmly on the ground."

THE SUMMER AFTER FOURTH GRADE was both the best and worst summer of my life. It was great because my cousin Denise stayed at my house during the week while she attended summer school. It was awful because of a misunderstood joke that would occur at summer's end. In between these highs and lows, I made two fateful decisions. First, I convinced Mom to cut my long, beautiful hair and give me a perm. Second, I begged my parents to take me to the optometrist. Although my vision was only slightly less than perfect, I talked them into getting me glasses.

Denise would go to school in the morning, get out at around eleven, then ride the city bus to the stop nearest our house. She would walk the mile to our house and arrive in time for lunch. That left us the rest of the day to play.

Denise was an angel when it came to entertaining me. There were beautiful woods behind our house, and my favorite activity involved going a little ways into the woods to a partial clearing. Small dogwood trees surrounded this little open area and Denise and I convinced each other that when we were in the clearing, no one could see us from the house. I should say that Denise went along with this fantasy to humor me, but I truly believed it. From our little clearing, we would play "Fatima." We would pretend to be shepherd children, and we would imagine that the Blessed Virgin appeared to us.

Even I realized this was just imaginary, but that did not stop us from performing pious acts. We would sing hymns dedicated to Mary or say the rosary. Because of the famous "miracle of the sun," we spent a lot of time looking directly at the sun hoping something would happen, sometimes convincing ourselves that just maybe it would start spinning. One time I looked up at a cloud formation and thought it resembled a scene from Our Lord's passion. I could make out what looked like Jesus being led to Pilate by the guards. It seemed that he turned and looked at me. I never deluded myself that it was anything other than an unusual gathering of clouds, but the idea of Jesus looking at me on his way to the trial before Pilate made quite an impression.

The rest of our days were spent tormenting my younger brother Gary or staging dance recitals. We would rehearse for hours, and there would always be a tap performance and a ballet performance. Never mind that neither of us had dance shoes of any kind, nor had we taken any lessons. We convinced ourselves that we were loaded with natural ability. When we had perfected our routines, we would invite family and a few neighbors to our evening performance. We always charged a "Yankee dime" for admittance. This was nothing more than a kiss on the cheek, but we considered ourselves quite clever.

When summer school was out, I went to spend one glorious week with Denise and her family. There were six children in the family including a sister, Claudia, who was a year older than Denise. We enlisted her in our devotion to Mary, and proceeded to spend endless hours playing May Procession while the two younger brothers spied on us and just behaved like pests. Aunt Bernice, Denise's mother, was a wonderful cook and she made the most incredible iced tea ever. Every night she made a huge pot of the stuff with halved lemons floating on top. At the end of the meal, we all clamored to get one of those pieces of lemon to suck on so that we could savor the tea to the last drop.

One night, Claudia, Denise, and I begged Aunt Bernice to let us camp out under the stars. She gave her permission and the next morning she built us a campfire and fixed breakfast over it. We had bacon, oatmeal, toast, and coffee. Even after all these years, I include it as one of my most favorite meals.

I MENTION THESE wonderful memories here because my life was about to drastically change. Two weeks before school started, Claudia, Denise, another cousin named Rose, and I spent several days at my grandparents' big farmhouse. At night, we would pair off to go to bed and then proceed to giggle until all hours with that person. The night before I was to go home, I was paired with Denise. As we were talking and being silly, I started clicking my tongue inside my bottom lip. Suddenly, Denise said, "Don't do that!" She seemed genuinely terrified and I timidly asked her why. "Don't you know you can swallow your tongue doing that?" she replied in an astonished voice. I had never heard of such a thing, but I was quite shaken with this information. Very quietly, I asked her what she was talking about. She went through a rigmarole of a story that had me convinced she was telling the truth. Then she rolled over and went to sleep. I stayed awake the rest of the night.

When my parents picked me up the next day, I was a changed person. Because I was shy, they did not realize at first that anything was wrong, but I knew. I felt that I had been betrayed or protected from the truth or worse. I could not believe that people were just going about their business with the knowledge that at any moment they might do the wrong thing and swallow their tongue. To make matters worse, and using twisted logic, I decided that, since this had been hidden from me for all these years, I could not trust anyone to tell me the truth. Even worse than that, I was afraid someone would confirm this truth. These factors made it impossible for me to talk to anyone about this.

The days that followed were a nightmare. I never slept on my back for fear that my tongue would just roll right down my throat. I could barely eat because I just knew that swallowing food might also mean I would swallow my tongue. For some reason, I decided that taking big gulps of liquid with each bite of solid food would be safer. This meant that I could never again taste a morsel of anything without at least a glass of water nearby. I endured all of this alone. However, I did have prayer. I kept begging God to give me the strength to help me live with this horrible revelation.

Outwardly, I really did not exhibit behavior that was that much different from normal. Although my eating habits had drastically changed, I was masterful at covering this up. The fact that there were four children in the family made it easier to do this. I was reasonably okay when I was up and playing but if I got still for even a moment the terror returned. I began losing some weight, but I had always been thin so it was not that noticeable. Mom did ask me a couple of times if something was wrong. Regretfully, I just could not bring myself to discuss this with her.

When I look back at the turmoil that I put myself through, I often laugh, but there was more to be gained than just a humorous memory. This experience taught me patience. It deepened my faith and ability to trust in God. It made me vow to be a vigilant parent someday in a way that only someone with a similar experience would understand. At that time, however, I just had to find a way to survive fifth grade.

A FEW DAYS BEFORE our much-anticipated postcards arrived, Ellen, one of our classmates, had several of the girls over for the day. She told us that her mother had heard that Sister Honoria was returning and that she would be teaching fifth grade. All of us got very excited and said how much we hoped to get her as our teacher. When the postcard arrived, I was disappointed to learn that I did not get Sister Honoria. The good news was that all of my friends were in my class. Our teacher was Mrs. Fonseca.

The day before school started, my older brother Clayton went to his high-school registration. The mother of one of his friends brought Clayton home, and he, a friend named Larry, and Larry's mom came in to visit for a while. Eventually, Larry, Clayton, and I went outside. I had a little crush on Larry so I was making a pest of myself, but for some reason, they let me play "Swing the Statue" with them. When it was Larry's turn to swing me around, he must not have realized how light I was because I went flying and came to the ground with a thud. Realizing that I was going to hit the ground hard, I put my hand out to catch myself and ended up breaking my arm at the wrist. The next day I went to the first day of fifth grade with a cast on my right arm, short frizzy hair, and glasses, not to mention a damaged psyche over the tongue-swallowing incident.

Mrs. Fonseca proved to be an interesting teacher from the very first day. She did not have a clue as to how to maintain discipline. I think she was actually just too idealistic in her expectations of us. She was brilliant and loved learning for its own sake. She incorrectly assumed that we were all there for the same purpose, therefore good behavior would be a natural occurrence. However, the class was huge and the boys in particular were beginning to assert themselves and exhibit macho behaviors. For their part, some of the girls were already beginning to see a future in impressing these wise guys. All in all, it was a lively group.

Our year began with the sad reality that many of our classmates in Sister Honoria's room would be leaving us soon. They were just waiting for the completion of a new Catholic school, St. Jude, which was being built across town. I realize now that by putting all of those students together, the administration was helping them wean themselves from us before they had to leave forever.

The new school year also brought us a new principal, Sister Rupertine. Sister Rupertine won my heart within the very first week of school. At that time, I was still riding the school bus home. The number of students who needed to ride the bus was too great for one trip. This meant that there were two routes, one leaving right after school, and the other upon the return of the bus driver from the first route. Those of us unfortunate enough to be in the second group had quite a long wait after school. The end of the school day was 3:00 p.m., and I only lived five miles away, but since I rode the second bus, I did not arrive home until 4:30 or 5:00.

While waiting for our bus, those of us on the second route had to wait in a classroom. During the first week of school, Sister Rupertine stopped by this room and asked why all of us were there. When we told her, she was truly astonished. She told us we should not have to wait, and she would see that the system got changed. Although I do not remember the details, Sister kept her word. I did not experience the new way very long, however, because in the meantime Mom had found someone living nearby who was willing to carpool, thus ending my school bus agony.

Because of my previously mentioned phobia about swallowing my tongue, a new problem arose. The fifth grades sat on either side of the church in the back. This meant that the walk up to Communion was a long one. For some reason, I had imagined that I could choke on my tongue during the simple act of swallowing accumulated saliva. Although I swallowed successfully throughout the day when my mind was otherwise occupied, in the line going up to Communion I would become so overcome with fear that I could not swallow. This would in turn cause me to panic and feel as if

I was going to pass out. After many days of suffering, I decided that I just could not take the stress anymore, and I stopped going to Communion.

This was a horrible decision. Mrs. Fonseca was a very spiritual person. She was also very practical, and could have been described as having one foot in heaven and the other planted firmly on the ground. She observed my behavior for several days, and then made her move. She knew how shy I was so she did not confront me face to face. Instead, just before time to go to Mass one morning, she told the class she wanted to talk to us. She explained that sometimes people stayed away from Communion because they thought that they were unworthy. She assured us that at our age, she did not think we had ever deliberately done anything that should keep us from receiving the Eucharist. She encouraged us to talk to a priest in Confession if we had any doubts about this. Then she emphasized what a privilege it was for each of us to have the opportunity to receive Communion on a daily basis.

I was devastated by this talk. I knew that now she assumed that I was not going to Communion because I thought I had committed some terrible sin. Now I had a real dilemma. If I started going to Communion again, she would reason that she had been correct and that, at the very least, I thought I had done something awful. If I continued staying away from Communion, I risked her actually talking to me about it. I decided that the only option I had was to go ahead and take that long, agonizing walk up the aisle to Communion. I hoped that if I did, she would eventually forget about the incident. If I did not, I knew she would pursue it. For the rest of that year, I stormed heaven with the petition that I not faint as I walked up the aisle. I began to look around and notice that all of the other students seemed carefree regarding the eminent danger before them, and I prayed for the maturity to imitate their bravery.

AT SOME POINT in the early part of the school year, it was time for the students going to St. Jude to leave us. The teachers allowed our departing classmates to come into Mrs. Fonseca's classroom and visit for a while on their last day. There was a lot of sadness mixed with teasing and promises to keep in touch. One of the guys who was heading to St. Jude was my little admirer, John Davis. His family had moved to Signal Mountain, which was much closer to the new school.

Despite my rebuffs, John still had a crush on me. On his final day at OLPH, he came over to my desk and asked me to autograph something for him. I was not a cruel person, but what I did that day remains one of the most unkind things I have ever done. I flatly refused to sign his book. Even as he persisted, I turned him down. I truly had no cruel intentions when I did this. I was just so shy that I did not want anyone to tease me about having a "boyfriend." Forty years have passed since that day, but I still regret my actions. How was I to know then just what a precious gift this innocent love was to me?

Because of her intellectual abilities, Mrs. Fonseca was a proficient teacher in all areas of study. We added the subject of history to our curriculum in fifth grade, and I loved it. In geography, we continued with the travels of the boy named Peter. I am not certain, but our first history course was probably American history, which meant that the geography for that year was more than likely that of the United States.

Mrs. Fonseca believed in giving homework to reinforce what was being covered in class. Although I had been used to having homework on a regular basis since third grade, fifth grade was much more demanding. Most weeknights I was up until ten or eleven doing my homework. Even though I enjoyed reading about Peter and his travels, I hated geography homework. It seemed to take forever, and often I would call a friend to ask for help.

Another subject that was new for us was science. Mrs. Fonseca truly seemed to delight in this area. She encouraged us in all sorts of scientific experiments. I remember one time putting a small glass bottle filled with water into the freezer. Mrs. Fonseca cautioned us to leave the top off. I remember being amazed after several hours when I checked the bottle and found that the ice that formed rose above the rim of the container. The next day in class, we discussed our findings and concluded that water expanded when frozen.

Another time, I remember we were studying clouds. She made a point to notice what types of clouds were visible each day, and sometimes we would all go outside to look. Mrs. Fonseca never missed an opportunity to instruct us, and her love of learning made a deep impression on me.

One final memory I have regarding science class was our brief study of astronomy. I loved going to the planetarium. Seeing the night sky projected onto the ceiling fascinated me. One day, Mrs. Fonseca gave each of us a little piece of thin, blue cardboard cut in the shape of a circle. It was about three inches in diameter, and it was called a "star clock." The months of the year encircled the outer edges of the circle, the way numbers do on a clock. In the interior of the circle, three constellations were represented with little punched out holes. By going into a dark closet and shining a flashlight under the cardboard, the little dipper, big dipper, and Cassiopeia could be illuminated on the ceiling. There was a pointer designating October as the starting place to determine the positions of these constellations in the night sky. I was thrilled to be able to take this mini-planetarium home with me.

MRS. FONSECA'S COMMITMENT to her faith was just as deep. When it became apparent that we were quite a rowdy bunch, she came up with a plan to encourage good behavior while also learning about our faith. She told us

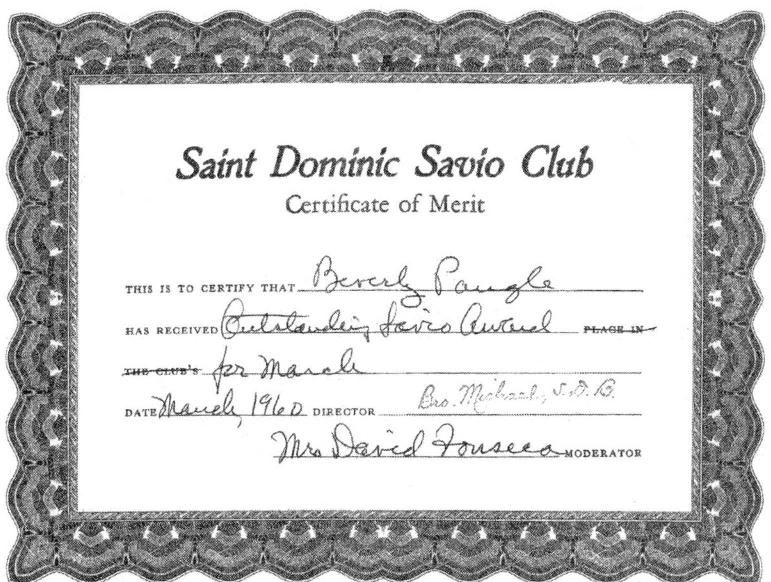

Saint Dominic Savio Club

Certificate of Merit

THIS IS TO CERTIFY THAT Beverly Pangle

HAS RECEIVED Outstanding Savio Award ~~PLACE IN~~

~~THE CLUB'S~~ for March

DATE March, 1960 DIRECTOR Bro. Michael, S.D.B.

Mrs David Fonseca MODERATOR

As a fifth-grader, Beverly received the Outstanding Savio Award for March of 1960.

about a young Catholic boy named Dominic Savio who had led an exemplary life. An organization had been set up in memory of this young role model. Mrs. Fonseca began a chapter of this club in our fifth-grade class. We read Dominic's life story and agreed to emulate him, and as proof of our intentions, we set up the club with officers and monthly meetings. As further encouragement, Mrs. Fonseca began giving out monthly "Dominic Savio Awards" to the student or students who most closely followed the tenets of this young man's life. I can remember the thrill I felt when I was recognized in this way during one of those months.

It was a tribute to Mrs. Fonseca's spirituality that as a lay teacher she was allowed to be our instructor of religion. She tackled this task with the same gusto with which she approached our academic subjects. More than that, she was an example of piety and fidelity to the teachings of the Church. I had known of her reputation ever since my toddler years because she and my mother had been in a Bible study club during that time. Mother would frequently remark not only on Mrs. Fonseca's wealth of knowledge about the Bible and church history, but also about her application of that knowledge in her daily life.

In her wisdom, Mrs. Fonseca knew that religion was sometimes a dry subject for children to tackle. She tried to be creative in her approach. She knew that at least among the girls, holy card trading was still the rage. Using this, she proposed a "holy card contest." Each student was to take his or her favorite holy cards and arrange them in a display. They would be judged according to attractiveness and demonstration of faith. Of course, as the deadline for the contest approached, I became sick. Since I did not have my entry ready, and had no ideas, I began to panic. Mom suggested the very simple idea of arranging the holy cards on poster board in the form of a cross. I remember that she convinced me to cut around my card of Jesus in the Garden of Gethsemene and put that at the top of the cross. I was astounded when I was at home recuperating and a friend called to tell me that I had won the contest. It seems that the fact that the intention of these holy cards was to lead us to Jesus and the fact that my display was in the form of the cross made it a theologically sound presentation.

It was during my years in grades three through five that I would love to surprise my parents with spiritual cards. These special occasion cards were made available to us at school. They always had beautiful religious artwork on the outside. Inside, there was a verse and a place to offer prayers of various types such as Masses, Communions, rosaries, etc. Years later, Mom confided to me the chuckle she and Dad got when they would open the card and find among the prayer offerings: twenty ejaculations. Of course, the double meaning of this reference was not suitable for me at that time and my parents were always appropriately grateful to me for my prayer offerings.

From the very first day of school, Mrs. Fonseca took every opportunity to teach us practical things, which we could use the rest of our lives. Three of these little lessons stand out in my mind. One of the first things she told us had to do with her technique for remembering facts. She told us to repeat the fact to be remembered three times and each time to picture writing this fact on our brain. I remember that she emphatically traced back and forth across her forehead as she gave this directive. We took the spelling of the word "environment" as our example. Three times we repeated the word, then spelled it as we "wrote it on our brains." To this day when I hear the word "environment," I think of Mrs. Fonseca. More important, I have used her technique all my life and it has never failed me.

Another valuable bit of information that she passed on to us was the importance of following directions. With her down-to-earth brand of humility, she related to us a story about an event that occurred when she was a newlywed. A dish she had prepared did not turn out quite right. When she lamented to her husband about it, rather than offer only sympathy, he had her go back over the steps she had taken to prepare the item. In doing this she had to admit that she had not read the directions at a critical point in the recipe, producing the bad result. As she told us this anecdote, she made sure to credit her husband with gently guiding her to the conclusion that following directions is not only imperative to a proper outcome, but always saves time in the end.

With the lesson about directions in mind, Mrs. Fonseca then told us another tale about her and her husband. This story is a little fuzzy in my mind, but the gist of it centered on the location of a rustic vacation spot situated near a beautiful lake. They referred to the body of water as "lost lake" because it was very difficult to find the way to this place. I remember that Mrs. Fonseca told her story with humor, and I am almost certain that her husband was the one who bore the brunt of teasing over the fact that he did not ask directions when they lost their way. She emphasized to us the importance of asking for help when necessary. Her story taught us that, as foolish as we might feel about asking for help, we could look even more foolish if we did not.

Sometime in the early fall when we were outside after lunch, some of my friends and I saw Mrs. Fonseca talking to Miss Merrill, the church secretary. We saw Miss Merrill eagerly showing something to Mrs. Fonseca, and being curious, we moved in for a closer look. What the secretary was showing her was a beautiful, blue crystal rosary. We immediately began "oohing and aahing" over this religious article, and Miss Merrill let us in on their conversation. She told us that she had ordered the rosary from an ad she had seen in *Extension* magazine. She allowed us to hold the rosary. When we did, we saw that it was quite exquisite. The large beads had teeny statues inside—at least that's what I thought I saw during the few seconds I was able to hold the treasure. I decided that it was the most beautiful rosary I had ever seen, and I was dying to have one.

That afternoon, when I got home, I burst into the house with the news about the rosary. I told my mom that I just had to have one like it, and since we had a subscription to *Extension*, I was certain she could get it for me. I told her it could be one of my Christmas presents. I did not know how to interpret the look on her face then, but having raised two children, I now definitely know what she was thinking. She was worrying that perhaps she could not get the rosary and then I would be very disappointed. She was also probably thinking that due to the nature of the gift, she would need to do everything she could to fulfill my wish.

When Thanksgiving drew near, Mrs. Fonseca suggested that we write a poem or essay about the holiday. Creative writing assignments were new to me, and I had trouble coming up with an idea. When I told my mother, she suggested that I write a poem about the feast from the turkey's perspective. "A Turkey's Thought on Thanksgiving Day" was the resulting masterpiece and Mrs. Fonseca loved it.

As the weeks went by, I brought up the rosary repeatedly. I did not get into details. I just constantly reminded Mom that I still very much wanted that rosary. She would say things like, "Honey, you might be disappointed," or "There might not be enough time to order anything." I never knew whether she was being honest or whether she was pulling a double reverse to throw me off the track, but in the back of my mind I just knew that she would come through. Of course, I was right. There among my many presents was a beautiful rosary that she had ordered from *Extension* magazine.

Christmas in fifth grade brought Beverly the soapstone rosary with the Litany of Loretto carved on the beads.

The only trouble about the rosary was that it was not the same rosary that Miss Merrill had shown to us. It was not a beautiful, blue crystal rosary. Instead, it was beige soapstone with the Litany of Loretto carved onto the beads. My heart sank when I saw it, but then I looked up and saw Mom eagerly watching for my reaction upon finding my prized gift. I squealed with delight as I looked at the rosary and pretended to chide her for making me think she could not get it for me.

She then told me the story of how she had searched the ads of the magazine until she found the rosary. She had remembered me telling her something about what was on the large beads of this rosary, and when she read the ad, it mentioned that the images of various Apostles were carved into the large beads. She knew she must have found the right rosary and she ordered it. As disappointed as I was at the time, I could never have told her then that it was the wrong rosary. Over the years, I have grown to treasure that rosary. On many of the beads, the carving has all but worn away from use. Someday, I look forward to passing it on to one of my children or grandchildren.

While books on Fatima had held my interest in fourth grade, in fifth grade something else caught my attention. I checked out a book from the school library about Marian apparitions in Beauraing, Belgium. These began in November 1932. Four girls and one boy witnessed the visions, and the message from Our Lady was much the same as that of Fatima. She urged the children to pray and make sacrifices. I loved this book, and it only served to increase my resolve to say the rosary each day. That Christmas I would receive another special gift, which would add to this devotion.

The summer before fifth grade, my older brother Clayton had worked on my grandfather's farm for most of his vacation. He earned a little over sixty dollars, which was a substantial amount for the time. At Christmas, we siblings usually exchanged gifts out of items that our parents had purchased and put our names on. This particular Christmas was different. Clayton took his hard-earned money and bought gifts for all of us. I was astounded when I opened my present to discover the most beautiful nightlight I had ever seen. The base was a music box that played "Ave Maria." It had a small drawer, just big enough to store a rosary. On top of the base was a statue of Mary with a bulb inside so that it glowed when it was turned on. Although Clayton and I still bickered with each other on a daily basis, receiving this gift was a turning point for me. It was the first time that I viewed my brother as a thoughtful person rather than just someone with whom I competed for attention.

My cache of Christmas presents also included three books. Mother fostered a love of reading in me from a very early age. First, she read to me every day before my nap when I was a toddler. Then she filled my life with books. In fifth grade the books I received at Christmas were: *The Fisherman's Ring,* a story about the life of Pope Pius X; *Young Girl of France,* a book about Joan of Arc; and *Pudsy Kelly's Follower,* a collection of poems that centered around the antics of a group of Irish boys, especially one named Pudsy Kelly.

When I first received these books, I all but turned up my nose at the Pudsy Kelly book. Sensing my feelings about it, Mom took it upon herself to bring this little book to life. I can still remember her enthusiastically calling me to her side to listen to one of the touching or humorous poems. Her excitement was contagious, and before long I would pick up the book on my own and enjoy its contents.

ONE THURSDAY AFTERNOON, after the Christmas holidays were over, I came home from school and went downstairs to skate. We had a huge basement with a smooth concrete floor that was a perfect surface for skating. Three steel poles served as supports for the steel beams in the ceiling. I would fly around these poles as fast as I could, sometimes catching one and swinging myself around at a dizzying speed. On that particular afternoon, I had a friend over to skate with me. We had the stereo on loud and were having a ball. I decided to do my trick of catching the pole as I sped toward it, but just as I got close to the pole, I looked back at my friend. In that instant as I turned my attention back to my stunt, I slammed my cheek right against the pole. The thud was so loud that Mom heard it upstairs. Although my cheek was quite tender, I was conscious and nothing seemed to be broken.

After my friend left, the rest of the evening progressed in normal fashion up until the time that I got ready for bed. As I brushed my teeth, I noticed that one of my primary molars was ready to fall out. Mom pulled it for me, and told me to bite down on a rolled up Kleenex to stem the bleeding. I went to bed that way, and in the morning much to my horror, I awoke with a pillow soaked in blood. Mom was a little alarmed particularly in conjunction with the skating accident, and she kept me home from school. My friend Beth was to have come home with me that afternoon to spend the night, and I convinced Mom to go ahead with that plan.

As the day went along, I began to feel ill. Normally I would have played this for everything it was worth, but because Beth was coming over, I did not want to let on anything was wrong. By the time she was dropped off by the carpool driver that afternoon, I was running a fever and beginning to cough. Quickly Mom realized that I was getting sicker by the minute, and she called Beth's parents and told them she would take her home after dinner. I ended up with a horrible flu and I was out of school for nearly two weeks.

This was probably the worst illness I had while I was in grade school. Mom spent hours reading *Heidi* to me in order to soothe my aching body. One night when everyone was asleep, I began screaming. My parents both ran into my room and later told me they were terrified at the sight of me. They flipped on my light and found me there in bed with my eyes wide open, screaming in terror. Apparently, I was still asleep and it took them a while to wake me and calm me down. I had experienced the worst nightmare of my life, but the details were absurd.

In my dream, I found myself in a huge, drafty barn in the middle of winter. In the center of the barn was a large piece of rectangular shaped concrete that was standing on end. It was about ten feet high and eight feet wide and it had one month in the calendar carved on it. It was my duty to hold this calendar up as it balanced precariously on one end. But that was not all. The barn door kept blowing open and a fierce, cold, angry wind blew into the barn. Somehow, I knew it was also my duty to keep this door closed. I spent the entire nightmare frantically running back and forth from the concrete block to the barn door trying to live up to what was expected of me. As I tried to relate the details of this dream, I had great difficulty. I found it impossible at that age to put into words the burden I felt.

Although I tried to tell my parents about this dream, I was unsuccessful at conveying why it was so terrifying to me. I am certain that it only appeared to be related to anxiety produced by my overactive imagination. In truth, I would discover more than twenty years later that this dream was in fact prophetic concerning my life, and what had been a scary event would become a comfort. It has become a sign to me of God's constant presence in my life.

The flu-like illness left me with a bad case of bronchitis. The cough lasted several weeks after I returned to school, and it sounded awful. To make matters worse, when I would begin coughing as the congestion loosened, I felt as if I was choking. This, coupled with my tongue-swallowing phobia, made me terrified during a coughing spell. One particular day, as this situation occurred in class, I was coughing and sputtering and tears were rolling down my cheeks. I know I appeared very frightened and one of my classmates noticed and yelled, "Mrs. Fonseca, I think Beverly Pangle is having a stroke!" Bless his heart, he was truly concerned, but for me the experience was humiliating. Mrs. Fonseca sent me out to get some water. After I calmed down, she let me call my father to come and pick me up.

When I look back on incidents such as this one, I marvel that no one made fun of me. I don't think I would have fared as well in the atmosphere of today's classroom. We smugly seem to think that we have come so far in the area of tolerance, yet sometimes I think we have come much further in the area of sticking our noses into the business of others for the purpose of being much more judgmental. Mrs. Fonseca was a very wise woman. She knew I was anxious about something, but she did not force me to confess to her.

In today's climate, she would have had the pressure of public scrutiny to such a degree that she might have felt compelled to elicit some sort of explanation from me.

In my case, that would have been inappropriate. I had to grow up and laugh at myself over my anxiety before I wished to share the experience with anyone else. I got through it on my own because of several factors. I had loving, conscientious parents, I had a firm religious foundation, and I had caring teachers who respected my privacy. Because I was aware of the inherent support which existed within these conditions, I was able to muddle through until I conquered my fears.

AS THE END of the school year approached, I continued to contract little illnesses. Finally, my pediatrician decided that I should enter the hospital for tests. There was a place called Children's Hospital in Chattanooga, but it was a large, dark-looking building and I was afraid to go there. Because I would soon be eleven, my doctor received permission to enter me into Memorial Hospital, which was run by Catholic nuns.

I was put in a semiprivate room with a twenty-one-year-old woman named Eunice. She was beautiful and very sweet. The nurses absolutely loved her, and many patients on our floor would roll down in their wheel chairs to visit her. She never seemed to mind that she had to be in a room with a child, and before I was discharged, she had one of her relatives bring me a little gift. I remember that it was a bracelet, but I no longer recall what it looked like. It was only after I got home, that Mom confided to me that Eunice probably had stomach cancer.

During my week-long stay in the hospital, I had many tests done. There was blood work and there were x-rays. At one point, a tube was inserted into my bladder. None of these tests bothered me. Then one day a technician came in and told me she was going to administer a test to measure my basal metabolism rate. She assured me that the test was painless, and that I would think it was nothing. Of course, she did not know about my phobia.

She explained the procedure, and when she told me that she would be putting a tube with a seal around it into my mouth, and then clamping my nose shut, I just about died. For some reason, this just intensified my fear of swallowing my tongue. She told me that they would be forcing pure oxygen through the tube, and she might as well have said that they were going to force my tongue down my throat. I was convinced that the rush of oxygen would do that very thing. I did try to be brave and endure the test, but I remember that whatever results were obtained were inconclusive. I can only assume that I began hyperventilating, and somehow threw the figures off.

Much of my experience in the hospital was very pleasant. Besides my wonderful roommate, I had a great new book to read. It was an unabridged copy of *Little Women.* I could not put the book down. My friend Catherine had already read it, and each day when she got home from school, I would call her to talk about what I had read that day.

Catherine's aunt was a nun who happened to be the head dietician at the hospital. On our food tray, there was a card to write comments. When I found out about Catherine's relative, I wrote Sister Francis Richard a little note telling her who I was. This occurred at the evening meal on the first day of my stay. When visiting hours ended that night, an orderly came around with a juice cart, and asked us if we would like a glass of juice. I timidly asked for grape juice, but apparently, the worker thought I said grapefruit juice and that is what I was brought. I tried very hard to drink the bitter stuff, but ended up leaving half of it when she returned to retrieve the glasses.

The next morning on my breakfast tray, was half a glass of grapefruit juice. I was sure that it had been saved from the previous night and that I was being shown that I must finish it. Just about the time that I was beginning to tear up, in walked a jolly nun who introduced herself as Sister Francis Richard. She brought me a beautiful holy card and a little pin depicting Our Lady of Fatima. However, the most wonderful thing she did was to ask me if there was anything she could do to make my stay more comfortable. I told her about the juice mix-up. Underneath she must have been chuckling, but she treated me with the utmost dignity. She personally removed the grapefruit juice sitting on my tray, and went and got me some grape juice. For the rest of my visit that was what I was brought.

MY CONFINEMENT in the hospital happened to coincide with our review week for the end-of-the-year diocesan exams. Mrs. Fonseca told Mother to tell me not to worry about this, and I took her advice. I did not study while I was in the hospital because my parents and the doctor thought it was important that I not have any stress. After the results of all of the tests were in, the doctor told my parents that physically I seemed to be fine, but that I was a very anxious child. They all decided that I just put too much pressure on myself, and that eventually I would become less nervous. This diagnosis meant that even less attention was put toward exam preparation. Again Mrs. Fonseca told my parents not to worry and that she would consider all things when the final grades came out.

Exams were grueling that year. For some reason, I had a particularly difficult time with the English exam. My friends told me afterward that Mrs. Fonseca had reviewed them heavily in this area. On the last day of school, there was an all-school Mass. At the end of Mass, Father Bush handed out report cards and we were all dismissed for the summer. I received my report card and quickly glanced down the last column of grades for the yearly averages. I was relieved to find that I had good grades in everything. Then to my horror I looked at the next to last column for exam grades. There permanently written on my report card was the grade of "F" for the English exam. I was stunned.

Because my younger brother had already gotten out of school a week earlier, I was the only one riding home with the lady in our carpool. When she got to the entrance of our neighborhood, I asked her to let me out because I wanted to walk the rest of the way. My eyes were stinging with tears as I closed her car door. For the quarter mile walk, the tears streamed down my cheeks. When I finally reached home, Mom was quite concerned when she saw me. I handed her my report card and blurted out my shame over the poor grade. Quickly, Mom looked over the grades and then said, "Oh, Beverly, for heaven's sake. You did not do well on one exam. Mrs. Fonseca told us not to worry and see here, she did not penalize you for the low exam grade. She just had to put down what you really made on it." With that statement I closed the chapter on fifth grade.

Chapter Six

"There had been an enormous shift in the development of my conscience that began in fifth grade. . . . My spiritual instruction both at home and at school was having an effect on me."

MY PARENTS ENJOYED going to construction sites and following the progress of new housing developments. My younger siblings and I loved to tag along and explore. Mom quickly learned to bring along a few damp washcloths and some towels in order to clean any mud or sand off our little bodies before we would head for home. During the summer after fifth grade, we made frequent trips to one site, but this one had a different purpose. It was the location of a new Catholic school that was under construction.

Although this school was approximately the same distance from my house as OLPH, it seemed very rural. I loved the feeling of driving "out to the country" to view the various phases as the new St. Stephen's Country Day School was being built. My parents talked about this project with much enthusiasm. As fall approached and the school neared completion, Mom asked me if I would like to go there with my brother Gary. She told me that there had been a request for volunteers, and she thought it might be something I would enjoy.

Mom's excitement was contagious. I was very shy and I loved my friends at OLPH, but paradoxically, I also enjoyed the adventure of change. I readily agreed to her suggestion. A couple of my closer friends also took up the challenge. The fact that a boy I had had a crush on since second grade also agreed to go did not hurt in making my decision.

St. Stephen's was not ready on opening day that fall. Temporarily, those of us planning to attend school there had to meet for our classes in a basement hall under the gymnasium at OLPH. Up until this time, the hall had been referred to as St. Stephen's Hall, but this name was changed, apparently because of the new school, to Madonna Hall.

Because of the small number of students willing to transfer to St. Stephen's, there were only four teachers assigned to the school. Each class was a split class. This meant that my class was a combination of fifth and sixth grades. This could have been a challenge for any teacher, but we were fortunate enough to have Miss Stone as ours. I am certain that we were her first teaching assignment, and I am still amazed at what a natural-born teacher she was. She was pretty and vivacious with a gift for discipline. She was also deeply spiritual, very kind, and very bright. She had high expectations for us, and she handled the split class as if this sort of assignment was a breeze.

As much as I liked Miss Stone, I did not like going to St. Stephen's. When we finally did move into the school, most of us still had to arrive at OLPH in the morning and ride a school bus over to the new school. I hated that. We attended daily Mass, but it was held on one side of the cafeteria. I missed my beautiful church at OLPH with its stained-glass windows. Finally, I just never really liked our principal. She did not do anything wrong that I recall. She just was not Sister Rupertine, whom I missed very much.

There were some comforting factors. One of the nuns from OLPH, Sister Bernard Louis, came to teach the first- and second-grade class. It was nice to see her familiar face. Father Bush would periodically come and quiz the classes, just as he had done at OLPH. As terrified as I was of giving a wrong answer, his presence added a sense of continuity. Also, Mrs. Guarde and Mrs. Pennebaker, two moms who had been girl scout leaders, continued as such with the remnants of our troop who were at St. Stephen's. Finally, our uniforms remained the same except for the emblem on our boleros that read "SSS" instead of "OLPH."

Beverly Pangle's sixth-grade picture with the SSS emblem instead of OLPH.

Academically, sixth grade went

smoothly for me. I fell in love with history that year. It was the grade-school version of *Western Civilization,* and I could not get enough of it. Miss Stone was very effective as a history teacher. When I attended college years later, it was her influence and that of Father Campion, my high-school American history teacher, that made me want to pursue history as a course of study.

We continued with the same curriculum that we had studied in fifth grade. The only aspect that was different was our religion book. In sixth grade, we moved on to the dark green *Baltimore Catechism.* This book followed the same format as the dark blue version from previous years. However, it was a more in-depth study of our religion.

THAT YEAR, for the first time in my life, I paid attention to politics. We all did. It was 1960 and John F. Kennedy was about to make history as our first Catholic president. I remember how proud I was to be Catholic. Chattanooga during that time had a Catholic population of about 5,000, compared to the total population of around 150,000. The Jewish population was even less than the Catholics. Most of the rest of the citizens were Protestant, with a high number of those belonging to various Baptist congregations.

It was not unusual for my father to find hate-filled literature tucked under his windshield wiper as he left work during the weeks leading up to the election. These pamphlets contained horrible things about the pope and many lies about the Church and what would happen if Kennedy were elected. Daddy would bring this propaganda home and laugh about the ignorance of those who would believe such things.

I would feel inflamed with Catholic pride. When Kennedy won, we were allowed to watch commentary on the election returns on televisions brought into our classrooms. That afternoon, I called my closest friend at OLPH and she told me that they too had been allowed to watch TV. Then she told me about the lone girl in the class who had been a Nixon supporter. As the rest of the class eagerly watched in jubilation, this poor girl buried her head in her arms and sobbed.

Miss Stone was nearly perfect, but she was human. Although she seemed to try to resist, she did have a couple of favorites in the class. There was a precious little girl in the fifth grade that she was obviously drawn to. Much to my dismay, this little girl seemed to like the sixth-grade boy who was my secret heartthrob, and the feeling seemed to be mutual. Miss Stone also thought highly of this young man, and for good reason. Both of these students were bright and attractive. I don't think any of us were really jealous because they seemed very deserving in a "who wouldn't be fond of them" sort of way.

For my part, I thought about John Davis a lot that year. I remembered how I had rebuffed him. Now I was experiencing unrequited feelings, and it hurt. I think I considered it some kind of justice, and in my heart at least, I made amends to John. I had not actually seen him since he went to St. Jude's School the year before.

There had been an enormous shift in the development of my conscience beginning in fifth grade. This was due to an accumulation of factors. My spiritual instruction both at home and at school was having an effect on me. My internal and lonely battle with the fear of swallowing my tongue was making me stronger in the area of empathy. Finally, in May of that year, I first heard about a man named Adolf Eichmann. My mother mentioned that this man had been captured and was to be brought to trial in Israel.

Every kid knew who Adolf Hitler was, even if only through silly depictions of him in cartoons. I considered him evil, but I had only a vague understanding of the reasons. It was the arrest and subsequent coverage of the trial of Adolf Eichmann that cleared everything up for me. Early in the fall of 1960, I was watching television one Saturday afternoon. Most children would have been outside playing rather than watching weekend daytime TV because the selections were not really geared toward children in those days. Sometimes, however, wonderful old movies would come on, and this led me to check out the programming that day. I became fascinated by what I saw on one of the channels.

The program was about the upcoming trial of Eichmann, which would take place the following spring. As a prelude, this particular presentation showed actual footage of concentration camps, crematoriums, and piles of dead bodies. The effect on me was chilling. I had never met a Jewish person, but as I watched the show, my heart was full of sorrow. I could not fit into my brain the idea that hatred of a people could have led to such devastation. Internally, I grieved for the children who lost their parents and for the children who lost their lives.

After that Saturday, I watched and read everything I could about Eichmann and the Holocaust. There were articles in magazines such as *Life* and *Look* that I would read when we visited my Aunt Carolyn. I scoured our encyclopedia for whatever information was available to me. The realization that these events had happened at all, much less in recent history, had a sobering effect on me. I wanted so much for this man to fully own up to his responsibility in all of the destruction. He looked like such an ordinary man. I wanted to see a monster, or at least hear from him that he had been temporarily insane. I spent most of that school year waiting and hoping and feeling crushed by my growing awareness of the potential for cruelty that is within all of us.

ALTHOUGH TRANSFERRING to St. Stephen's had taken me out of the loop with most of my friends on a daily basis, somehow we managed to maintain contact. I enjoyed the little group of friends who were with me at the new school. I was particularly happy that my friend Patsy, whose mom was one of the scout leaders, was there. Patsy was hilarious and kept us all in stitches. Occasionally, she would spend the night at my house. We would usually spend all day Saturday roaming through the woods behind our house. No one suspected that I was combating my phobia each day. I appeared to be a normal child with the right balance of social, family, spiritual, and academic life.

One weekend during that fall, my cousin Denise, her younger brothers, and parents stopped by to visit. For some reason, we got out our Hula-Hoops. Maurice, the older of the two brothers who were there, challenged me to see who could keep one going longer. In a situation such as this one, I was never shy. I relished this sort of competition. I was able to maintain my Hula-Hoop in motion longer than Maurice, but then I got cocky. I suggested that I could keep it up for 1,000 rotations, and then I proceeded to do just that. Years later, only the pain of childbirth compared with the abdominal distress I experienced as a result of my foolishness.

One other comical yet very painful experience occurred that fall. We had a large yard with many trees surrounding our house. One Saturday, my dad and mom were out raking some of the leaves, which was an enormous undertaking. To make the task a little easier, they decided to use the wheelbarrow to carry loads of leaves to the edge of the backyard. They would then dump them down an embankment, which led to the woods behind our house.

My younger brother, one of our next-door neighbor friends, and I decided it would be fun to jump in the increasingly bigger pile of leaves and roll down the embankment. We were merrily engaged in this activity when suddenly the neighbor boy stood up and went running and screaming over to his house. His mother came out of their house, sized up the situation, and yelled something over to Mom. My brother and I, still oblivious to what was going on, thought the boy was being silly and we kept up our activity. Mom came running over to us and excitedly told us that the leaves were full of yellow jackets and for us to get out of there quickly. It was too late. Gary and I had each just gotten our first sting, and we both began yelping. Mom and Dad rushed us into the house, peeling off our clothes and killing the yellow jackets as they shoved us toward the bathroom and into the showers. When everything had settled down, I had been stung twelve times on my abdomen, and Gary had at least that many stings on his body.

For a few days in late fall or early winter of sixth grade, we had a young substitute teacher. She was the older sister of a girl who was a year ahead of me. I remember a couple of things about this young woman. First, she liked history, which meant she did not skimp on that lesson each day. More important, she told us about a dedicated young doctor she knew. It seems that he had been giving his life in service to the people of Vietnam. I am not certain, but I believe this young woman might have worked with him. As she spoke about the young doctor, she became very sad, and she told us that we should pray for him. His name was Tom Dooley, and he had terminal cancer. In January of that school year, I heard on the news that Dr. Tom Dooley lost his battle with cancer and died. I thought about the young substitute and her compassionate request for prayers for this man who had made such an impression on her. Her example was one more lesson by a layperson living out her faith.

✎ I REALLY LOOKED forward to Valentine's Day that year. Miss Stone had made it clear that if anyone brought a Valentine for one person, there would have to be one for everyone from that student. I was so hoping that the boy I had the secret crush on would give out valentines. I would then be able to pour over the one he sent me for an inkling of sentiment.

The afternoon before Valentine's Day, my younger brother and I got into a huge argument. In exasperation I punched him on the arm and then quickly turned away. He was very fast and swiftly came back at me with his fist. I am certain he was aiming at my back, but I turned around and leaned down toward him just in time for him to punch me in the eye. Hurriedly, I put my hand over my eye and went outside bawling for my mother. The eye had begun to swell and the pressure of that against my hand made me think that my eyeball was falling out. It is comical now to envision me running up to my mother and a neighbor screaming that Gary had knocked my eye out.

Mom had a look of terror on her face as she pried my hand away from my eye. This quickly turned to relief when she realized that it was only the area around my eye which was swelling. She took me in to put an ice pack over the eye and to try to calm me down. When I had composed myself, she really let Gary and me have it for causing such a commotion. I was completely humiliated to see the black eye that was developing. I did not want to go to school the next day, but then I remembered it was Valentine's Day and love won out. I did not want to miss the chance of receiving that special valentine. When the appointed time for the distribution of the cards finally arrived, I was disappointed to realize that in fact the one I worshipped from afar had not brought valentines.

At some point in the school year, Miss Stone showed us her engagement ring. We felt very important to have been let in on this excitement. I do not recall if her wedding took place during our spring break or after school was out for the summer. I do remember how much she looked forward to it and how romantic it all seemed to me.

Sometime in the spring, Miss Stone received a baby rabbit. Again, she brought us into the excitement. She told us she would have to name the bunny, and we would be the ones to help with the task. That afternoon, after lunch and recess, we got down to the serious business of coming up with something appropriate. Four or five names were suggested, and Miss Stone wrote each one on the board. She considered each one until she finally decided that the rabbit would be called Brigit.

AS I REFLECT and write about these grade-school memories, I cannot help but notice the way I feel. There is a difference in my feelings toward the nuns, as opposed to the lay teachers. Miss Stone is a good example of this. She was wonderful, and I loved having her for a teacher. She did not display the cattiness that is often found in young teachers. Sometimes, a young teacher is eager to fit in with the students at their level. This desire often leads to behaviors that hurt the less popular students. Miss Stone was not like that in any way. She was conscientious and compassionate in her dealings with each one of us, and she was remarkably mature. I attribute this in part to her strong faith.

However, I realize that my feelings are even deeper regarding the nuns who taught me. I can only assume that their complete commitment to God provided them with a power and aura that was different from even the best lay teacher. I had a profound respect for these women. I knew that during the summer most of them were attending school so that they would be better prepared to do God's will in their teaching endeavors. I knew that they had given up their families, and that they had no say in where they were assigned. I knew that they endured wearing dark, hot habits as symbols of their commitments. I even vaguely realized that they were always under glaring scrutiny by those who were suspicious of the Catholic faith.

All of these factors gave me a sense of gratitude toward these women that has not diminished over the years. The dwindling number of teaching sisters is more frightening to me than the extinction of a species of animal. We are allowing a very special manifestation of God's grace to go unused if young women do not continue to inquire into a possible vocation to the religious life. Today, in my parish, we pray for this intention. I trust that these petitions will be answered.

In May 1961, Adolf Eichmann's trial began. I remember seeing news reports of the proceedings. As he sat there in his booth with his earphones on, he reminded me of a contestant on a game show. He looked that ordinary to me. His assertion that he was following orders was sickening to me then. Years later, I would reflect with a more mature mind and realize how we all have the tendency to rationalize our behavior, and that would be even more frightening to me than this man who had done so much evil. I understood those who said, "Never forget," and "Never again."

At the end of the school year, my parents asked Gary and me if we would like to go back to OLPH. We eagerly said yes, as did many of the others who had transferred that year. I left St. Stephen's with a light heart. It had been a good year; I looked forward to summer, and in the fall I would be back in familiar surroundings with more of my friends.

Chapter Seven

"We accepted death as a part of life.
We experienced initial shock that someone our age
could have died, but we also experienced
the reassurance that our faith gave us."

My mother is a remarkable person. As I complete this book, she is going strong at eighty years of age with ideas and projects constantly in the works. Life in the summer of 1961 was no different for her. By that time, she had been president of her Bible study group and our large neighborhood garden club. She had worked tirelessly with the Legion of Mary, the Altar Guild, and the Home and School Association. Most recently, she had successfully sold Tupperware, but that summer she was beginning to get restless again.

For many years, OLPH had been without a kindergarten. Mom got the idea that she would be a good kindergarten teacher. She had not been to college, but in those days a degree was not necessary to teach at that level. Her youngest child was four and a half, and Mom reasoned that Mary Elaine could go with her each day. Daddy was supportive of the idea, and when Mom presented it to the decision-makers at OLPH, they were delighted. I was ecstatic when she told me she would be teaching there in the fall.

Seventh grade at OLPH was departmentalized. For English, spelling, reading, and history, we had a brand new teacher named Mimi Wilkerson. She also taught the girls physical education (PE) once a week. Sister Rupertine taught us math and religion, and Coach Waters taught science. Once a week, Sister Leonine would come in to teach music, and we occasionally had an art class taught by a parent named Mrs. O'Rourke.

For various reasons, I liked having several teachers. Because I was quiet and shy, I felt that the hourly turnover of teachers would make it more difficult to focus any attention on me. Additionally, this sort of scheduling made me identify more with my friends in the neighborhood who went to public junior high schools. Of course, the difference was that my neighbor friends moved from classroom to classroom. We stayed in one room, and the teachers moved.

When I told Mom about my young English teacher, she told me that she had already met her, and that Miss Wilkerson was the daughter of one of my father's business associates. This poor young woman had no idea what she was getting into when she accepted her teaching assignment. There were approximately fifty adolescents in the classroom. She had never taught before, and she was not Catholic. I have often regretted what a horrible example we were for her, and what a frustrating experience she must have had that year, her only year at OLPH.

As for my mother, she was having a ball with her first teaching experience. As difficult as it is to believe, kindergarten programs in 1961 were mostly set up for children to play, color, and hear stories. My mother, with no experience and no degree, decided that she would establish a readiness program in her kindergarten. I was thrilled when she began asking me to tell her about my academic memories of first grade. I filled her in as best I could about printing, phonics, and numbers, and she built a curriculum based on that and other ideas she had. For its time, it was truly innovative.

Mom's first kindergarten class was huge, nearly fifty children. She was alone without an aide, and by the end of the first week, she had completely lost her voice. For several days until she could talk again, Sister Rupertine allowed me to miss school all morning and I became Mom's voice. I relished this time, and it cemented in my mind that one day I would become a teacher.

I WAS VERY HAPPY to be back at OLPH, but things were changing. Cliques were beginning to develop and there was cattiness and infighting, as well as rivalry between cliques. These kinds of conflicts disturbed me, and I resolved not to be a part of any group. Very often, this put me in the middle of things, and to some people I was considered a mediator. If one person from a particular group happened to be temporarily on the outs with that group, often the rejected person would hang around with me during that time. Occasionally, my attempted neutrality would backfire. Both sides of a dispute might expect me to side with them, and if I tried to find validity with both points of view, I would often end up with the two groups mad at me. This was definitely a part of adolescence I did not like. On the other hand, it did begin to prepare me for the real world.

My older brother was a junior in high school and he played on the football team. We teased him that he warmed the bench more than anything else. Nevertheless, ever since his freshman year, we had supported him as a family by attending his games. I absolutely loved Friday nights in the fall at those football games. My friends and I would leave our parents in the stands, and go sit near the high-school kids. The boys in my class would pay attention to the game, but for the most part, the girls watched the cheerleaders. We all dreamed of getting to do that ourselves someday; we soaked up the cheers, and learned every movement, and every word.

During halftime at one of the games that year, some friends and I went to the concession stand. I wanted some hot chocolate, and when I got to the stand, I realized that I did not have enough money. I borrowed some from a friend and got my drink. When we returned to the bleachers, I went to where my parents were sitting to get the money I needed to pay back my friend. My mother had a very disturbed look on her face, and I asked her what was wrong. She said, "Did you not hear the announcement that was just made?"

Fearing something like the announcement of World War III, I cautiously shook my head no, and asked her what the announcer had said. I was stunned with her reply. The announcer had asked for prayers for the Davis family. It seemed that one of the sons, Mike, who played on my brother's team, had lost his brother that afternoon. I could not believe what Mom was telling me. John Davis had died that day!

I was in shock. The rest of the game was a blur. When it was over, we went to the open house as usual to pick up my brother. This particular evening, it happened to be held at St. Jude's school. That was John's school. When we got there, the mood was somber. People were speaking in hushed tones, and some information trickled down to my friends and me. According to what we heard, John had been born a "blue baby." There was discussion that he was Rh-negative. Whether this was incidental to the cause of his death, I do not remember. Whatever his congenital difficulty, when John was born there was no way to remedy the problem. The day he died, he had come home from school and told his mom that he felt great. It was such a beautiful day he told her that he was going out to ride his bicycle before going to the game. It was during this outing that his heart gave out and he died.

I do not remember if anyone else from my class went, but I insisted that my parents take me to the funeral home. There was an open casket, and I was struck by the peacefulness of the body of this little boy. He seemed to be sleeping, and I think I remember that his glasses had been placed over his closed eyes. John's father came up and spoke to my parents and me. He was so kind to me, and his words resonated bittersweet in my heart when he told me how fond John had been of me.

Sister Lena was there too with some of the other nuns. She came over and comforted me by telling me she was certain that John went to heaven immediately. She added that she had known him to make the nine first Friday devotions. She also told me that now I would have a very special friend in heaven that could pray for me in a special way. I loved Sister Lena for focusing my attention on John's goodness and on our eternal destination.

For several days, the talk in our classes turned to John's death. We did not have counselors come in to help us deal with this event. Rather, we focused on the loss for his family. Different teachers helped us in different ways. Sister Rupertine approached the matter from spiritual and charitable angles. Coach Waters helped us greatly by explaining John's congenital problem in a way that we could understand. We accepted death as a part of life. We experienced initial shock that someone our age could have died, but we also experienced the reassurance that our faith gave us. Mostly, we thought of John's parents and siblings and the loss they were feeling. Reaching out to comfort them helped us heal, too.

In the years following John Davis's death, even until today, I have thought of him often. Each time he comes to mind, I say a prayer for him and for his family. Many times over all of these years I have felt alone or troubled and I have talked to him and asked him as a special friend to intercede in my behalf. I agree with Sister Lena that he is a little saint. My ongoing spiritual relationship with him over the years has kept clear what we had been taught about sainthood. We are all called to sanctity and those who go before us continue to help us in eternity just as they helped us as friends on earth.

AS THE YEAR PROGRESSED, I continued to pick up bits and pieces of the trial of Adolf Eichmann. I don't ever remember talking to any of my classmates about the horrors that this man committed, but the topic of his trial did come up a couple of times. Coach Waters was always well versed on topics of current events and I seem to recall a student mentioning Eichmann and Coach then going into some detail about the trial. Within my own heart, I continually thought about the millions of Jewish people sacrificed. I would be an adult before I really knew about the deaths and experiments that were performed on the physically and mentally challenged, homosexuals, Catholics, and so many others. In seventh grade, however, it was enough to know that Hitler had wanted to exterminate entirely the people of one religion.

I had been wrestling for two years now with my tongue-swallowing phobia. It was beginning to recede, but still lurked in my subconscious. One day, when I was absent from school, I called a friend late in the afternoon to get my homework assignments. In passing, I asked her what went on that day. She said, "Nothing much, except, oh yeah, Coach Waters saved a boy from swallowing his tongue!

"What do you mean?" I gasped. She then related the story of how a student had been on the playground and had been hit in the Adam's apple with a softball. Apparently, the boy was having difficulty breathing and Coach had gone over and pushed on his throat to keep him from swallowing his tongue, according to my friend. Well, I did not understand at all what she had just described to me. I am now certain that it was a jumbled reconstruction of the events, but at that time, it only renewed my terror. I was too frightened to question her further, and I was amazed that she told me the story so calmly. Didn't people care that at any moment they might swallow their tongue?

I REALLY LIKED Miss Wilkerson. She was that young, sweet teacher that every shy, gawky girl needs in adolescence. Mom needed to be at school early to greet her students, and that gave me the opportunity to walk in with Miss Wilkerson. She is the only teacher I ever talked to about fashion. She was so compassionate toward me that I forgot about my shyness. One time, I remember telling her about a favorite dress that I had gotten during the summer. It was a white dress with a pleated skirt and it was made of a fabric called sharkskin. However, I did not know what the fabric was called until I described it to Miss Wilkerson.

She became very animated when she talked to me about it and said, "Oh, it must be sharkskin. I love that fabric! It is the best thing to travel with because it just does not wrinkle." It was just such ordinary conversations that meant the world to me. My feelings of awkwardness melted away when we talked. It was one of those rare times in my life as a twelve-year-old when I felt totally myself. I treasured the thank-you note that Miss Wilkerson wrote for the Christmas gift I gave her that year.

Miss Wilkerson was also a capable teacher who was academically sound. However, discipline was her nemesis, as it has been for many first-year teachers. She told us during the beginning of the school year that we would start giving two-minute talks each six weeks. I was consumed with fear. The assignment for the first talk was to select an object and describe it. I agonized over what object to pick. One Sunday, as we were driving home from a day at my grandparent's farm, I commented for the hundredth time on a billboard that I loved. It was an ad for Coca-Cola and it pictured three icy coke floats. I would crave ice cream every time I saw this billboard. Suddenly Mom said, "Beverly, why not give your talk about that advertisement? You could call it 'A Tempting Taste Treat.' "

Using Mom's brilliant suggestion, I easily wrote the little speech. The real hurtle was delivery. As expected, I was terrified. Miss Wilkerson had emphasized that we should hold only one index card with some essential phrases. I might as well have been asked to walk a tight rope fifty feet up without a net. However, I knew that all of us were in the same boat. My fear was having everyone's eyes on me, with or without complete notes. Something magical happened with my presentation of that talk. I was convincing in my delivery. The students began to focus on what I was saying rather than on me. When I finished, they were just as hungry for an ice cream float as I was each time I saw the ad. Miss Wilkerson raved about the speech and gave me an "A." She pointed out that I had made my object appealing, and that I had delivered the speech clearly and with expression.

It would be nice to think that this cured me of my shyness, but it did not. This was just one wonderful moment that I would treasure in my memory. If anything, it had a delayed effect. Years later, when I had to make presentations in college, I used what I had learned that day to capture the audience's attention, and thereby take the focus off me. I still freeze up with fear at the prospect of speaking in front of a group, but at the same time, I know that I can survive it.

It was not Miss Wilkerson's fault, but I hated history that year. We were required to study Tennessee history in seventh grade, and I found it incredibly boring. I was not alone in this thinking and the class as a whole floundered. I regret now that I did not pay closer attention to the subject because my mother's father had been prominent as a state senator in some of that history. It could have been a source of family pride if I had become more knowledgeable.

ONE DAY, as Miss Wilkerson was leaving our classroom and Coach Waters was coming in for science, he must have realized that he needed to ask her something. He went running after her saying, "Mimi! Mimi!" We were laughing hysterically when he returned. We had never heard a teacher referred to on a first-name basis, and we began whispering that Coach had a crush on Miss Wilkerson. This was only in our pathetic imaginations. In reality, he was married to a vivacious, petite woman named Hazel who had borne him six children, and still managed to keep her figure. However, we did not care about those details that day. It was too much fun to tease him about his slip in protocol.

Coach Waters was an excellent science teacher. He had taught biology at the Catholic high school, and we were lucky when he took the job offer at OLPH. I was afraid of him, but without reason. He was fair, and I don't believe he ever raised his voice to me personally, and not that often to the class. If we showed particular interest in something we were studying, he was always willing to go into more detail than what the book offered. He dissected a frog for us, and told us about pithing a frog for the purpose of observation.

One day, Coach brought in a bottle of carbon tetrachloride. I no longer remember the exact circumstances, but in the course of the class period, one of the boys was holding the jar. He took off the lid and breathed in the fumes. The student became woozy and mild panic ensued when he passed out. Once the crisis was over, Coach Waters lectured us on the dangers of assuming that chemicals were safe. It was not suggested that the boy had been sniffing the stuff to get high. Rather, he carelessly took a whiff of it and was overcome. For a while his nickname was "Carbon Tet."

Ever since I can remember, the students complained about having to wear uniforms. In seventh grade the girls had a minor reason to celebrate regarding this matter. In years past when we went to church, the girls had worn either beanies or berets that matched the uniforms. In seventh grade we were allowed to wear chapel veils. They could be either black or white, and they looked like flimsy doilies held in place on our heads with bobby pins. To us they were a monumental improvement.

As the year progressed, girls began wearing circle pins as a fad. The pins were just plain gold or silver circles, but most of the girls in seventh and eighth grades had them. As simple as these pieces of costume jewelry were, they were not quite innocent. If worn on the right side, it indicated the girl was a virgin, but if worn on the left, she was not. I did not have a circle pin, but I thought they were pretty and I certainly wanted to be in on the trend. Unfortunately, my knowledge of the word "virgin" only extended to the Blessed Virgin Mary. I had never analyzed those words, but knew that if applied to Mary, they had to be good. I knew what blessed meant, and I vaguely understood that virgin referred to the fact that Mary had never "known" a man, whatever that meant.

Armed with these loose facts, I went home and blithely told my mother that I wanted a "virgin" pin. Innocently, I had used the nickname that they had been given. Calmly, Mom asked me exactly what I meant by a "virgin" pin. I explained to her the significance of the position of the pin when worn, and she was no longer calm. She gave me a crash course in the full meaning of virginity, and what a priceless gift it was. She was outraged that virginity was being treated in such cavalier fashion through this fad.

It goes without saying that Mother was not about to get me a circle pin, but I never dreamed her next course of action. She went to school the next morning and talked to Sister Rupertine about it. Most of that school day was spent in turmoil. Sister came to the seventh-grade classroom and selectively called students out in the hall for questioning. I was called in the middle of those being questioned. When I faced Sister, she told me that she had called the others to find out what she could, but mostly to disguise the fact that she wanted to talk to me. She then had me go over the same details with her that I had gone over with my mother.

Sister Rupertine was clearly appalled and saddened by the connotation of the pin. The students in the seventh and eighth grades were told to stay after school in order to deal with this matter. At the end of the day, the boys stayed in the seventh-grade classroom, and the girls went over to the eighth-grade room. I do not know who spoke to the boys other than Sister Rupertine, but it would have been either Coach Waters or one of the priests. Sister talked to the girls too, but she also asked Mrs. Holt to speak to us. Mrs. Holt was a parent who sponsored the Junior Legion of Mary for the seventh and eighth grades.

I was deeply affected by Sister Rupertine's talk. It was apparent that she was sorely disappointed in us. She was also disappointed that somehow the teachers and the parents had failed us. The pins were forever banned because of their hidden meaning, but it was obvious that Sister was much more concerned about our loss of innocence. She tried to convey what we were losing by trying to grow up too quickly. She told us that although she was certain that we were all still virgins, she was distressed that we would essentially trivialize this fact, or even worse, tease that we were not.

Sister Rupertine loved us so much and as I write this, I am filled with sorrow. Many students and parents regarded Sister as interfering and too strict. In actuality, she was just extremely farsighted. She knew what awaited a world that gave up its childhood. She feared for our immediate spiritual safety, but also for the spiritual well-being of the future. I have always had complete trust in Sister Rupertine and her wisdom because her sincerity and holiness were unmistakable. Like many prophets before her, she was largely disregarded.

Some of my friends suspected that I was the one who had opened this can of worms, but I never let on that I did. I knew that the information about the pins would have eventually made its way to adults who cared, and I knew that it had never been my intention to reveal anything anyway. If I was guilty of anything, it was naiveté. I realize that by today's standards this incident seems silly, but I am still grateful for its lesson. Mom would appropriately emphasize chastity to me at home, but having this reinforced at school was a good thing.

WE WERE DEFINITELY a rowdy bunch. One day, when the boys were out of the room at PE, Miss Wilkerson gave the girls an assignment and told us she had to leave the room for a moment. She clearly told us not to talk. She had not been gone more than a couple of minutes when a low buzz began. A girl turned around and asked me a question, but I shook my head "no" in an attempt to make her realize that I was following Miss Wilkerson's instructions. I immediately went back to work, but the talking in the room grew progressively louder. Apparently, Sister Rupertine heard the commotion and angrily entered the classroom. Just as she was chastising us, a very embarrassed Miss Wilkerson returned. Miss Wilkerson told Sister how disappointed she was that we had misbehaved and said that she had left us with an assignment and a warning to keep quiet.

Sister Rupertine took a moment to size up the situation and then she asked if there was anyone in the room who had not been talking. She told us that if we had not talked, we should stand up. Never dreaming that I would be alone, I stood. The girl in front of me turned and indicated to me and those around me that in fact I had talked. I genuinely felt that my head nod was only a polite and legitimate way of brushing off her question. I knew I had not actually talked to this girl, so I remained standing. Sister then directed me to sit and she began lecturing us.

The theme of Sister's talk was disrespect and disobedience. She asked Miss Wilkerson to leave the room while she spoke to us. She told us how disappointed she was in our behavior regardless of who our teacher was, but especially since we had shown this example to a non-Catholic teacher.

She talked to us for ten or fifteen minutes and then she told us what our consequence would be. That afternoon instead of having fun during PE, we would do strenuous exercises the entire time. That is, everyone except me. She said that since I had not been talking, I would just sit and watch.

The forty-five minutes of PE that afternoon were excruciating. I sat in a folding chair at the edge of the gym floor and watched as my classmates did crab walks up and down the room. They did jumping jacks, and sit-ups, and every other imaginable exercise, whining and groaning all the while. They were not too happy seeing me sitting on the sidelines either. I think that in her wisdom Sister Rupertine put me there because if I really had not been talking, she wanted the girls to be reminded that they too could have avoided this. On the other hand, if I had lied, it would be humiliating for me to watch my class suffer while knowing I did not deserve immunity. Of course, I knew that there was the little discrepancy of the head nod, but in my conscience, I knew that I had completely lived up to the spirit of what had been asked of me. If anyone bore me any lingering ill will, it was not apparent in the days that followed this incident.

This punishment had some lasting side effects. In general, the behavior of the girls improved. For me, I realized that I could do the right thing even if those around me did not, and sometimes this could mean that I would avoid painful consequences, yet not take pleasure in the pain endured by others for their mistakes. By adhering to Miss Wilkerson's instructions, I had been forced to choose sides against my peers that day. I credit my parents for lovingly instilling within me deep respect for my teachers. This respect kept me from talking, but one thing did always puzzle me. I knew that there were other girls in my class who were equally respectful. I wondered if they had actually been talking on that particular day, or if they knew that they would be in a very small minority if they stood up.

That day was just one of many when a nun, priest, or Catholic teacher would remind us of our responsibility of being a good example in everything we did. This lesson stuck with me more than any other. I clearly got the message that example was the best method of evangelization. We were taught that it was not enough to proclaim our faith. We were called to live it at every moment.

SISTER RUPERTINE was a bright woman and an excellent math teacher. She was strict and demanding, but fair. It is not unusual to find math teachers who are knowledgeable in their field. It is refreshing to find those who can transfer that knowledge to their students. Sister Rupertine was one of those rarities. She was able to put across math concepts in a way that I could easily understand.

Because of her deep spirituality, Sister Rupertine was also a wonderful religion teacher. One could not miss her commitment to us concerning our spiritual well-being. We were typical twelve-year-olds who snickered at many things related to authority, but I don't think anyone would have questioned Sister's sincerity. The ache in her heart over our welfare was often apparent in her lined face. Sometimes, when she spoke to us with exasperation in her voice, I would feel sorry for her. Almost immediately, I would then picture Jesus on the way to Calvary, telling the women not to weep for him, but instead to weep for themselves.

Occasionally, our religious instruction was supplemented by visits to our classroom by Father Miller, an associate pastor. Father Miller was a tall, thin priest who could be very stern. Most of the time, I remember him as having a dry sense of humor. We were on our best behavior when he was in the room because we sensed that he had a temper. For the most part, he just questioned us in detail about what we should have learned from the catechism, and occasionally he told us humorous stories. I still did not want to be called on by him, but at least I did not sit in his class with my knees knocking the way I did around Father Bush.

Sister Leonine came in once a week for music. As rambunctious as we were, I don't remember our class ever giving her any trouble. I know that she never raised her voice. She was beautiful and serene. Her quiet reserve must have woven a spell over us. We looked forward to music, although I don't remember much about the course. This was not due to a deficiency on Sister Leonine's part. I had begun taking piano lessons that year, and I now confuse what I learned in the classroom with what I learned at my private lesson.

Art was a different matter. We only had this class sporadically. True to form, I was absent on the first occasion that Mrs. O'Rourke came to teach the class. By the time she returned, I discovered that I was one step behind on the vase-painting project that she had begun. We each had a dark green, glass vase. At the prior lesson, Mrs. O'Rourke had demonstrated how to paint flowers on a vase. Everyone else already had a few white flowers painted on their vases when I got mine that day. I began to try to catch up, but Mrs. O'Rourke stopped me. It seems that I was trying to represent a flower with four petals. She told me that just as she had told the others earlier, the flower must have an odd number of petals. She said that this was true for all flowers. I never checked out the accuracy of this fact, but I also never forgot the lesson. Even today, I would not dream of drawing a flower with an even number of petals.

During the winter of 1962, the school sponsored a pancake supper. In order to promote this event, a poster contest was held. We were not required to enter, but the winner would receive two dollars. I was dying to win that contest, and told Mom I wanted to enter. My difficulty was that I could not think of anything unique enough to be eye-catching. Leave it to Mama to have the answer. We knew that since "Aunt Jemima" brand pancake mix was very popular, most of the posters would probably have her picture on them. Mother said that she thought we should go in that direction also. To make my poster interesting, I should draw a large "Aunt Jemima," but use fabric for her clothing and bandana. Mom found just the right materials in her scrap bag, and I set to work. I put a dialogue bubble above "Aunt Jemima's" head and had her saying something about the pancake supper. Except for the cloth which added dimension to the poster, it was quite simple.

The next day, I took my poster to school. There were only about ten or fifteen entries in my class. We put our names on the backs of our posters so that the judges would not be influenced, and then lined them up in the back of the classroom. The two nuns who taught first grade were the judges. The entire class sat quietly as the two women perused the entries. It seemed to take an eternity, but finally Sister Rupertine came in to announce that I was the winner. I was thrilled with the two dollars, but I was even happier with the artistic validation. I was a frustrated artist because, although the desire was there, skill was definitely lacking. This accomplishment gave me hope. Not long after winning, I convinced Mom to purchase for me the John Gnagy "Learn to Draw" kit. I was certain that I was on my way to artistic greatness.

THE YEAR ROLLED ALONG uneventfully. In the spring most of the talk turned to our anticipation of eighth grade. We could not wait to be "top dogs" with all of the privileges that entailed. For the girls there would be the opportunity to be a cheerleader, and on rainy days we would monitor the classrooms of the younger students while their teachers ate lunch. The boys and the girls would usher at Communion time, get to spend an hour in eucharistic adoration on the first

Beverly Pangle in seventh grade.

Fridays, and get to sponsor a school-wide Halloween party. It would be a very exciting year for us, and that made the last few days of seventh grade seem to take an eternity.

On May 31, my thirteenth birthday and just a few days before school was out, Adolf Eichmann was put to death. He had been found guilty at his trial in Israel, and received the death penalty. Although I have never been in favor of the death penalty, and at that time cringed at the thought of it, I knew that the crimes this man committed were barbaric. I wondered if the survivors of his victims felt relief now. In my heart I knew that nothing could make up for the atrocities he commanded or allowed to happen. I have never forgotten the images of the Holocaust that I saw as I followed Eichmann's arrest, trial, and execution. The impact went beyond the treatment of the Jewish people and for me extended to those of all religions, races, or nationalities. I made a commitment then to live my life with love and tolerance in my heart for all of humanity.

Chapter Eight

"I will always be appreciative for the experience of having my beloved Sisters of Charity of the Blessed Virgin Mary present in my life at such a crucial time of my development."

I SAVORED THE FACT that I was now an eighth grader. I could clearly remember how grown-up the students in eighth grade had seemed when I was in first grade. Our classes were departmentalized just as in seventh grade, but that year we had many new teachers. Coach Waters was back to teach us science and Sister Rupertine returned as our principal as well as our religion and math teacher. Mrs. Smith and Mrs. Friend were two new lay teachers, and Sister Harold and Sister John Phillip were new for us also. Sister Leonine returned to teach music once a week, but she also came to us daily for spelling.

Mrs. Smith was an elderly, non-Catholic teacher who taught us history and penmanship. She was very refined, but seemed ancient to us. There were approximately fifty students in the one eighth-grade classroom, and we gave Mrs. Smith fits. She was an excellent history teacher, and I enjoyed the United States history we covered that year. In penmanship, she repeatedly warned us that we should hold our pens correctly according to the Palmer method, or we would be sorry in our later years of life. I never mastered this technique and now I think of her as my stiff fingers just do not want to cooperate when I need to write something in longhand.

Mrs. Friend, our other new lay teacher, was Catholic. She only came to school in the afternoons and she taught us reading. She must have gone home with a headache every day because we were awful to her. She just didn't have the knack for discipline. Years later, when I became a teacher, I thought of Mrs. Friend often because I, too, was lacking in this area.

Mrs. Friend was constantly catching some student chewing gum. This was a major offense in the school and particularly so in her classroom. Her standard comment was, "Do you have enough for everyone?" When the culprit said no, she would then tell the student to take the gum out, put it on his or her nose, and stand in the front of the room. One day she caught a boy named Bobby chewing gum. When she asked him the usual question, he told her that, yes, he did have enough for everyone. Mrs. Friend was momentarily startled, then laughed, and asked him where it was. He told her it was in his locker in the back of the classroom. She instructed him to pass it out and he went back, opened his locker, and revealed multiple packages of Doublemint. We each got a piece, and Bobby was forever a hero.

As humorous as the gum incident was, I always felt sorry for both Mrs. Smith and Mrs. Friend. They were very good teachers and they did not deserve the treatment they got from our class. Many times during the school year, Sister Rupertine would have to lecture us sternly regarding our general behavior. Often, the class as a whole would have to do punishment writing, which I absolutely hated. In exasperation one day, Sister Rupertine assigned us to write an apology letter to Mrs. Friend rather than the standard "I will not talk in the classroom" two hundred times. By this point in the school year, I had become fed up with the lectures and punishments. I decided to point out in my letter that there were some of us in the class who were trying to do the right thing, yet we were lumped together and punished with those who misbehaved. I do not remember how I phrased things. I just know that I felt that I had worded the letter with strong language.

Just as I finished my letter, Sister Rupertine told us that when we were through we should take it up to her to read, and if she approved, we would then take it across the hall for Mrs. Friend to read. I panicked a little because I was worried that my letter was not in keeping with the apology mode. Timidly I took it up to Sister. She read it and then much to my surprise told me what a wonderful letter I had written and that I should take it across the hall and tell Mrs. Friend what Sister had said about it as I handed it to her. I wish I had a copy of that letter because I think it was probably the earliest example of my standing up for myself, and I must have done it in a diplomatic way. I do not know if my words had any effect on the situation, but we never again had group punishment writing from Mrs. Friend.

Sister Harold, our new English teacher, was incredible. I left grade school with a solid background in grammar because of her. She was a tall, thin young nun with a sharp, dry sense of humor. She did not mind laughter in her classroom, but she had no trouble whatsoever controlling her students. Although I really cared for Sister Rupertine, I believe that Sister Harold was my all-round favorite grade-school teacher. Oddly enough, even though I have so much recall of events surrounding other teachers, I draw a blank when I try to narrow my focus in that way with Sister Harold. I remember feelings rather than specifics. I know that she was resourceful, compassionate, knowledgeable, and fun-loving. She possessed the grace in a classroom setting that only skilled teachers acquire.

Having said all that, I cannot think of one example to back up any of this. I believe that I was totally mesmerized by her ease in the classroom. Rather than concentrating on individual episodes, I drank in her entire persona and that's what remains in my memory. Sister Harold became the yardstick I used to measure against myself when I became an English teacher. Because of her, I knew what a good English teacher was. Very quickly, I realized that I was not one. Although I knew my subject matter and I loved my students, I was not suited for the classroom. Sister Harold's example cleared that up for me and inadvertently led me back to school for my counseling degree.

I do have one humorous memory of an incident in Sister Harold's class that had a lingering effect on me. One day, she called on a student to answer a question. The girl gave an incorrect response. When this was pointed out, the embarrassed student turned red. Sister Harold noticed this, smiled at the girl, and said, "Wiggle your toes, and you won't turn red." I heard this and took it to heart. I also had the habit of blushing, and I was eager to keep it from happening. In an effort to do so, I developed a lifelong habit of wiggling my toes. Although the fear of blushing subsided years ago, to this day I often wear out a pair of shoes at the big toe areas. It seems I still unconsciously wiggle my toes during stressful situations. When I see the little hole beginning to form at the top of a shoe, I always think of Sister Harold and chuckle at my foolishness.

ALL OF HER STUDENTS loved Sister Leonine. She demonstrated an inward beauty that only enhanced her natural physical beauty. She was tall and graceful with a very gentle sense of humor. During music class that year, I particularly remember singing in rounds. We did not sing the usual "Row, Row, Row Your Boat," but rather things we had never heard of before. One of the songs was called "Zumgali." We had classes on music theory, too, but the corny, unusual songs that broke up classroom monotony were what I remember most.

Sister Leonine taught us spelling too. We probably thought that she would be a pushover, but she was much too conscientious for that. Throughout my grade-school experience, my teachers exhibited high expectations for all of us, and Sister Leonine was no exception. Gentle and tenderhearted as she was, she never compromised her high standards with regard to learning.

When we had Coach Waters that following year, he was just the same as he had been as our seventh-grade science teacher. He actually seemed to enjoy us. I would not realize until my own teaching experience many years later what a gift he had. In my work experience, I found the twelve- to fourteen-year-old age range very frustrating to handle. Unlike me, Coach Waters was up for the challenge. He had a knack for knowing just how intimidating to be without scaring us. He also understood that getting a little off topic every once in a while could breathe life into a class. He always stuck to things that were educational, but not necessarily related to the particular science lesson of the day. He never strayed from his lesson plan for long and my foundation in science was very solid because of him.

One day, Coach Waters called on me to read from our science textbook. The section we were reading dealt with some aspect of animal life. One of my sentences included the words: lions, tigers, and leopards. I was a good reader, and I had no difficulty getting through the passage. When I had finished, Coach Waters, with a devilish grin on his face, asked me to reread the sentence with the list of animals. I did this and he laughed and said, "Yes, you did it correctly this time. When you read it earlier, I was wondering what a 'LEO pard' was." The class, including me, laughed hysterically. Apparently, in my nervousness, I had pronounced "leopard" in a way that would rhyme with "leotard."

Sister John Phillip was a knowledgeable art teacher. She did burst my bubble a little regarding the John Gnagy "Learn to Draw" kit. Although I had no real artistic talent, I could follow the directions in the kit and draw the things presented. For some reason, as the year progressed, it was decided that along with a few other students, I would enter a citywide art contest. No one at school had ever seen my attempts at the Gnagy system, but I decided that my rendition of the Hispanic youth wearing a poncho and in the foreground of a pueblo-like building would be the perfect entry.

Those of us entering the contest had to meet Sister John Phillip on a Saturday in the school cafeteria to work on our projects. When I showed her my rough sketch, she was clearly not impressed. She told me it looked silly to have the large drawing of the boy with the tiny building in the background. She suggested that I just do the boy and leave it at that. She also had some suggestions for improvements, but that was my downfall. I could merely copy what I could see. I definitely could not improvise. Not wanting to let her down, I worked hard and did my best. We did our final versions in chalk and Sister sprayed them with a protective coating. They were sent to a local art gallery for the judging. When I did not even win an honorable mention, I hung up my artistic ambitions. In truth, Sister John Phillip had gently led me to the realization of my limitations.

Sister Rupertine came back that year filled with enthusiasm. The "new math" was all the rage, and she had prepared all summer in the methods to teach it to us. We learned how to multiply and divide in a completely different way from what we were used to and we kicked and screamed the whole time. As conservative as she was, Sister loved innovations in learning. Our lack of enthusiasm must have disappointed her, but she never gave up on us.

One day, as she was teaching a new concept, I could almost feel her anxiety over the fact that we were not catching on. Suddenly, without warning, she called on me to figure out a solution to a problem. Up until that moment, I had been struggling for understanding, but magically my mind opened and I realized that I could comprehend what she was teaching us. I answered correctly and have never forgotten the feeling of that on-the-spot accomplishment. Not only did I learn the math concept, but I also found out that it was not necessary after all for me to repeat answers over and over in my head before volunteering. It was quite an epiphany.

Sister Rupertine was equally as committed in her approach to us in religion class. She was genuine in her concern for our spiritual welfare, and never missed an opportunity to teach us a practical lesson. Numerous times she would write the word “self-discipline” on the board. Then she would practically implore us to recognize the significance of obtaining it in our lives. If this had been the only weapon in our character arsenal that she had taught us, it would have been worth having her for a teacher.

Sister Rupertine was relentless in her insistence upon the relevance of self-discipline. She even told us a joke on the subject. It went something like this: There was a man who lacked self-discipline. This fact was well known throughout his town. One day, the man saw a fine horse that one of his neighbors owned. He offered to buy the horse. The neighbor really did not want to sell it, but based on the other man’s reputation, the horse owner decided to have some fun. He made a proposal to the man. If the man could say the “Our Father” without interrupting himself, he could have the horse. However, if he stopped before the prayer was over, he would have to pay the neighbor what the horse was worth, but not receive it. The man who wanted the horse thought that this would be easy, so he readily agreed. He began, "Our Father, who art in heaven, hallowed be thy name. Thy kingdom come. . . . Hey, by the way, does that horse come with a saddle?"

The class got a kick out of Sister's story. For one thing, we were very surprised by her use of humor. She was usually so serious when she discussed these things that we were charmed by this deviation from her pattern. The story made an impression on me and has stayed with me all of these years. Often, when I have been tempted not to live up to some commitment or another, I have thought of this silly little joke and put myself back on course.

THE FIRST BIG EXCITEMENT in eighth grade was the selection of the girls' cheerleading squads. Every girl in eighth grade was allowed to be a cheerleader, but because there were so many of us, we had to have four squads. One day during the first few weeks of school, Sister Rupertine picked four girls who would each be the captain of one of the squads. I was one of the four selected. The other three girls were also good, relatively shy students. We went to the front of the classroom and took turns selecting girls to be on our squads.

Although I normally abhor this method of selection, I felt at the time that Sister was trying to give several of us who were conscientious an opportunity to elevate this to more than a popularity contest. I took this seriously and did not select my close friends or the most popular girls in my class. I mixed up my choices and did not wait until the end to take some of the so-called "undesirable" girls. I do not think that

I was alone in the way I handled things that day. All of us involved in the selection process were kind. Not everyone who was chosen was happy at first with the team they were on, but with the first opportunity of actually getting to cheer, these feelings quickly dissipated.

I don't know how anyone else in my class felt about another privilege we had as eighth graders, but I know I enjoyed it immensely. On rainy days or days that were severely cold, students could not go outside during lunch. In order to give the teachers their usual break, eighth-grade students were assigned to monitor the classrooms of the younger students. I loved being assigned to the first- or second-grade classrooms. The memories of the eighth-grade monitors when I had been in first and second grades were still fresh. These students were always so kind to us. The good ones would read us stories or play games. Sometimes they would even answer questions about themselves. I elevated them to celebrity status and vowed to imitate their example when I reached eighth grade.

Curiously, as much as I looked forward to this, I only remember one particular day. I was assigned to Sister Lena's fourth-grade class. She had both boys and girls in her room that year and as luck would have it, my younger brother Gary was one of her students. The situation was a bit embarrassing for me, but it must have been pure agony for him. There was a part of me that relished being in charge of him in an official capacity.

Father Bush and Father Miller had been transferred at the end of the previous school year. In the fall of eighth grade, we greeted two new priests. Father Niedergeses was the new pastor and Father Hanghian was our associate pastor. Sister Rupertine decided that there should be an assembly for the entire school to acknowledge our new priests. She asked my mother to be in charge of a little program for this purpose, and she wanted it to involve students at every grade level. Mom had proven herself gifted the year before by putting on a wonderful little play within the kindergarten graduation ceremony. She was thrilled that Sister trusted her with this new undertaking. When she went to Sister with her idea, it was well received. Sister told her that I should do the part assigned to an eighth grader. Mom was pleased, but I was terrified.

The program was quite simple, but effective. A student from each class in grades kindergarten through eight had a placard with a letter on it. I came onto the stage first carrying a placard with a capital "W." I walked to the far end of the stage and said, " 'W', 'W' is for wishes. Father Niedergeses and Father Hanghian, the eighth grade greets you both with best wishes and a promise of being dependable, loyal, and cooperative at all times."

Each participant in turn came out and stood next to the previous person with the card, reciting his or her part. Grades one through four had two classes each, which meant that there were a total of thirteen participating students. When all of us had finished, we spelled out the message, "Welcome to OLPH" across the stage. Everyone seemed to get a kick out of it, and since we were out of class for the assembly, the students enjoyed it most of all.

AROUND MID-SEPTEMBER, Sister Rupertine brought up the subject of the annual eighth-grade sponsored Halloween carnival. In a very tired voice, she mentioned that she was thinking about doing away with this event. As she looked around the room and saw our disappointed faces, she changed her mind, but she told us we would have to be very cooperative if she gave permission to proceed with the project. I am certain we all sincerely agreed to this, and Sister immediately began ordering the candy and prizes for the games. Our work would come later.

In the meantime, the topic that was most pressing was ballroom dancing. A lady named Mrs. Howell had a dance studio across town and for several years eighth-grade students from OLPH had gone to her on Saturday nights for dance lessons. Sister Rupertine was not thrilled with this. She had already cautioned us that we should not be having "boy/girl" parties, and although Mrs. Howell was perfectly respectable, Sister seemed to have her reasons for why we should not take lessons at her studio. There was a Catholic woman named Mrs. Garland who lived near the school and who decided to begin giving these lessons. Reluctantly, Sister gave her approval to Mrs. Garland whose lessons were in her home.

Most of the students opted for Mrs. Howell's. A very few, mostly those who lived near the school, went to Mrs. Garland's. I truly respected Sister Rupertine, but I found her concerns unwarranted in this circumstance and I convinced Mother to allow me to go to Mrs. Howell. In a matter of two or three weeks, several of my friends who had begun at Mrs. Garland's joined me. These dance classes were excruciating for me. The boys lined up on one side of the room and the girls on the other. Mrs. Howell placed herself in the middle and taught us the various dance steps. We learned the fox trot, waltz, cha cha cha, calypso, bossa nova, and the bop.

After teaching us the steps to a new dance, she would tell the boys to get a partner and then there would be a practice dance. This was the agonizing part. A few of the bolder boys would go and select one of the "popular" girls, but most of the boys just stood around until Mrs. Howell poked and prodded each one into asking someone to dance. I may never have been the last to be asked, but it was too darned close for comfort. To make matters worse, parents gathered about fifteen minutes before the lesson was over and were able to peer at us through a window in their waiting area. Mom always seemed oblivious to the fact that some boy was being forced to dance with me. Instead, she would just focus on the fact that she did see me dancing with so-and-so. Again, Sister Rupertine had been wise. I was not ready for this activity, and would have saved myself a lot of humiliation by not participating.

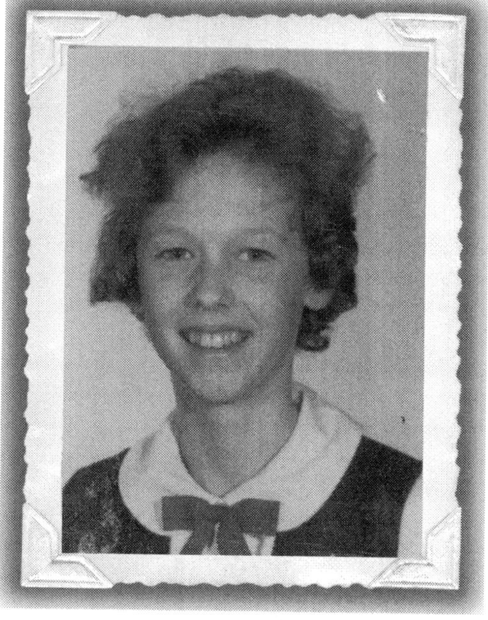

Beverly's new hairdo for her eighth-grade picture.

At some point during the second six weeks, it was time for school pictures. The weekend before, I got the insane idea to have a new hairdo. I begged Mom to cut and perm my hair. I just knew this "makeover" would transform me and release the raving beauty that lived within me. I wanted to be able to capture that for posterity. Without going into any detail, I have included the resulting picture on the preceding page.

As the week of the Halloween Carnival arrived, we went into high gear. Madonna Hall was transformed from a dismal basement into a festively decorated den of fun and games. We set up booths with cakewalks, fishponds, fortune telling (using the magic eight ball), Coke and popcorn, and various other delights. There was a haunted house in a room at one end of the hall and a place to watch short movies and cartoons in a room at the other end. Sister Rupertine had ordered an assortment of stuffed animals, candy, and trinkets to serve as prizes for the participants at the booths.

Two to four eighth-grade students ran the various activities in each booth. The students from the other grades dressed in costumes and for a couple of hours in the afternoon there was mild chaos in that hot, sticky hall. I remember being excited and repulsed at the same time. It was noisy and there were too many people crammed into too little space as far as I was concerned. On the other hand, it was delightful finally to be one of the ones in charge. At day's end, most of us met our responsibility to clean up Madonna Hall. Sister Rupertine looked exhausted or worried or both. After all the planning, all the hard work before, during, and after, we did not break even. Sister mentioned to the little group that had gathered around her that this was probably the last Halloween Carnival.

As the time to begin practicing for the Christmas program approached, all of the girls wondered who would be selected to play the part of Mary. Finally, Sister Rupertine announced that it would be Maggi. There could not have been a more appropriate choice. We had gone all through grade school together, and she was consistently good and kind. Maggi had dark brown hair, which she wore in a pageboy, and beautifully expressive, dark brown eyes. True to her nature, she was genuinely humble to learn that she had been chosen. Maggi's family moved away at the end of that school year. When I saw her almost twenty years later, she looked remarkably the same, and she had remained that sweet, loving person that I had known before. When we were in eighth grade, she had made Sister Rupertine's selection task easy.

Sandy, another girl who attended OLPH all eight years, was somewhat of a contrast to Maggi. My first memory of Sandy was from first grade. She lived in one of the houses behind the school property and her best friend at that time was a cute little blonde girl named Linda. On the particular day of this initial memory, I must have been waiting for the school bus to return from the first route. Whatever the reason, Sandy, Linda, and I were playing on the steps that led up to the front doors of the church. I remember that Linda talked about the fact that her mother was very sick and I felt sorry for her. Soon we began talking about more pleasant things and Sandy told me that I was invited to her upcoming birthday party. She said it would be that Saturday at her house. At the time I did not know exactly where she lived, and I asked her. She pointed and brightly said, "Over there, the house with the roof on top!" Linda and I giggled and from that day on, and that remark, I decided Sandy was very clever.

I did go to her party, but Sandy and I were never close friends. Her crowd grew up a little faster than I did, but I always felt she had a tender heart. When we were in eighth grade, the clique situation had only intensified. I was feeling increasingly uncomfortable with myself when I was with my peers at school. I am certain that this was also the case for many of the girls. Incredibly, even with the "pack mentality," there were several slumber parties that year to which all the girls in the class were invited.

It was during one of these parties at my friend Helen's house that Sandy demonstrated her thoughtfulness. She was probably at the peak of her popularity at the time. As the night wore on, some of the girls became catty with each other. At some point, Sandy looked over at me and in a voice loud enough for anyone in the room to hear said, "Beverly, you know, you are all right!" Any shy child knows what a boost it can be when someone who is more outgoing recognizes her existence. This was what I received from Sandy that night.

Toward the end of that year, Sandy and two other girls would end up getting into quite a bit of trouble over an unfortunate series of pranks they pulled. The other two girls had to finish the school year at two other Catholic schools. Sandy stayed and finished at OLPH. My only other encounter with her came when we were sophomores in high school. My dad dropped off the two younger children at OLPH and then took me to school. One morning I noticed Sandy on the corner after we left OLPH. She was waiting for the city bus to take her to our school. I mentioned to Daddy that she was in my class, and being the unselfish person he always was, he asked if we should offer her a ride. She readily accepted and got into the backseat of our car. I had the radio on and the next song that was played was "The House of the Rising Sun" by the Animals. I reached over and turned the radio up and said, "Oh, I love this song." As I said this, I looked at Sandy and she had an amazed look on her face. Eagerly she told me that she really liked it too. I realized that she found it somewhat fascinating that I would listen to and enjoy the same music that she liked.

I don't think I ever talked to Sandy again after that day. We just didn't cross paths. Sometime between our tenth and twentieth high-school reunions, I learned that Sandy had died a tragic death. Turning to my wonderful Catholic faith, I began praying for the repose of her soul. Often since then I have heard "The House of the Rising Sun" played on one of our oldies stations. At those times I always offer up another prayer for her soul and for the family she left behind. She had shown me her tender heart so many years before, and I always pray that she has received God's mercy.

IN THE VERY EARLY SPRING of eighth grade, one of the women's church groups planned a luncheon. They wanted to have a fashion show with some of the ladies plus some of the eighth-grade girls. I was one of the girls selected to do this and I was both terrified and thrilled. We each modeled one outfit. Mine was a beautiful party dress. It was made of satin with a dark floral pattern. There was a dark green satin cummerbund around the waist. I thought the dress was exquisite and even though I am sure we could not afford it, I convinced Mother to let me keep it.

When we dressed for the fashion show, we were allowed to wear lipstick. This was an incredible concession on Sister Rupertine's part. The show itself was not nearly as traumatic as anticipated. We just quickly modeled the clothes from the stage and then casually walked among the tables where the ladies were having their lunch. When it was over, we changed back into our uniforms and went to class. Very quickly on our heels was Sister Rupertine, who immediately called us out into the hall. She informed us that the lipstick had only been for the fashion show. She then directed us to the restroom where she told us to wipe every trace of it off. This was the closest I had ever come to getting into trouble since that day so many years before when Catherine and I had missed the recess bell in first grade.

Soon after the fashion show, there was a time when I really did think that I was in trouble. Sister Rupertine had become increasingly exasperated with the behavior of the whole class. We had been lectured and punished to no avail. I remember it being a very stressful time. I thought our conduct was deplorable, but I was weary of the conflict of personally trying to be conscientious while the room was often in chaos. We seemed to be fine when any of the nuns or Coach Waters was in the room, but the presence of other lay teachers did not command our respect. In addition, if for some reason a teacher briefly left the room, pandemonium reigned.

I remember one time when one of the boys had to use crutches. When a teacher stepped out of the room, one of the other boys grabbed a crutch and somehow managed to hang it on top of one of the fluorescent light fixtures dangling from the high ceiling. This seems mild, but with over fifty bodies wiggling and giggling and generally restless, everything that occurred snowballed into turmoil. Someone, usually Sister Rupertine, would soon storm in and scold us. I often went home from school in the afternoon with an awful migraine headache.

As if the conduct itself was not bad enough, there also seemed to be somewhat of a rebellion going on regarding the school uniforms. This brings me to what I feared was my impending doom. Girls were required to wear navy blue skirts and boleros, white blouses and socks, and a red grosgrain ribbon tie. The boys had to wear navy pants and ties, and a white shirt. For a while Sister Rupertine had been scolding us for neglecting to wear complete uniforms. It seemed to be deliberate behavior on the part of some students, particularly regarding the ties. Finally, she threatened us with some form of individual punishment if we did not comply with the dress code.

A day or so after this warning, as luck would have it, I inadvertently left my tie at home. I realized it the moment I sat in my seat that morning and I was panic-stricken. I decided that the only course of action would be to face the music and tell Sister before she noticed it herself. I was terrified as I approached her and mortified at the possibility of being put into a category with the flagrant violators. Quietly I told her my dilemma. She looked at me with the kindest eyes and said, "Dear, I know you did not deliberately leave your tie at home. My admonition has been to those who habitually do this. Now, do not worry about it anymore and do not do it again." She was so gentle with me, yet she did make certain that I not stray as a result of leniency, so she added that final phrase. I loved her all the more that she thought so much of maintaining my reliability that she used even that as a lesson.

AS WARM DAYS APPROACHED, I finally got my opportunity to spend an hour before the Eucharist. On first Friday's of each month, the Eucharist was exposed in the monstrance on the altar. For twenty-four hours there was perpetual adoration of the Sacred Host. Adults would volunteer to come to the church in increments of an hour in order that someone would always be present adoring Jesus in the Eucharist during this twenty-four hour period. During the school day, it was a privilege of the eighth graders for two of them each hour to make this visit to the church.

My turn came in May. I do not know who was assigned with me, but I am certain it was one of the boys. I remember sitting on the left side of the church facing the altar. The little windows of the church were open and I could hear the sound of a lawnmower and smell the newly mown grass. I knelt some of the time, but mostly I sat and thought about this opportunity. I knew that eventually when I lived on my own, I would make a point of spending time like this in a quiet church. Even at that age I had a sense of awe at the privilege of grace that drew me to the Eucharist. I knew that I had not done anything to deserve this longing, and I was grateful for this gift.

Although it was only one hour in my existence, the effects would last a lifetime. Often during summer vacations while in high school or college, I would convince Mom to go with me to early morning Mass. I loved being there without the distraction of a crowd. Later when I married, I would go to daily Mass whenever possible. I now belong to a parish that has a perpetual adoration chapel. Sitting before the Eucharist is the most healing thing that I could ever do. The refreshment found there is for the body, mind, and soul. I am grateful not only to God for the grace to do this, but to my wonderful nuns who, along with my parents, guided me to know of God's grace in the first place.

As the school year was ending, we had a sports banquet. I did not participate in any sport other than that little bit of cheerleading, but Sister Rupertine wanted me to be one of the people who made a speech. I was chosen to give the speech for Mrs. Colosia, our PE teacher. The banquet was held in the school cafeteria, and as with any other event we had many rehearsals. The speeches were given rather informally. When my turn came, I just had to stand at my place and deliver my little talk. I do not remember what I said, but I do remember that the entire evening was so low-key, I was not nervous. In fact, that is probably the only time in my life that I have spoken publicly without a case of the jitters beforehand.

One afternoon a couple of weeks before school was out, two friends and I decided to stay in at recess and grade papers for one of the nuns. We were in our classroom, and when we had finished we began acting silly up at the podium. After one girl had said some funny stuff, I decided to break out of my shell. I went up to the lectern. I got a very serious look on my face and said, "I just want to take this opportunity to thank the faculty for giving me the Outstanding Girl Award." The girl who had spoken before me turned on me and angrily said, "Just what makes YOU think that you would get that award?" I remember feeling so humiliated because never had I actually dreamed I would get that award. I immediately said, "But I was only teasing. I think Maggi will get the Outstanding Girl Award." This was the truth. She was the perfect choice as far as I was concerned. But when I said this, the girl was even more indignant and it was then that I realized that she was dying to have this honor. The three of us were very quiet until the bell rang and the other students came back inside.

When the last day of school finally came, we had an afternoon assembly in the gym. The whole school was there, as well as many parents. Those of us in the eighth grade who were receiving honor pins sat on the stage. When all of the honor pins and perfect attendance pins had been given out

Eighth Grade Certificate

Diocese of Nashville

This Certifies That

Beverly Ann Pangle

of

Our Lady of Perpetual Help, Chattanooga

Name of School City

has satisfactorily completed the Course of Studies prescribed for the Eighth Grade by the School Board of the Diocese of Nashville, and therefore is entitled to receive this certificate.

In Testimony Whereof our signatures are hereunto affixed this

1st day of June 1963

Sister Mary [illegible] B.V.M., Principal

Rev. James F. [illegible], Pastor

Rev. John A. [illegible], Superintendent

+ William L. Adrian, Bishop of Nashville

June 1, 1963, Beverly Ann Pangle graduates eighth grade.

to students from all grades, it was time for the awarding of the Outstanding Boy and Girl. A man and a woman from the DAR (Daughters of the American Revolution) and SAR (Sons of the American Revolution) were on hand to present these medals. I was dumbfounded when my name was called out as the recipient for the girl's award. I remember the thunderous applause, which touches me to this day. Years later, when Sally Fields gave her much-parodied Oscar speech, I understood exactly how she felt. They liked me. They really liked me! I looked out into the audience and there was my dad sitting with Mother. Knowing in advance about my award, he had gotten off work early as a surprise to be at the assembly. His words so many years before had come true.

Briefly, we returned to our classroom after the assembly. There I found my peers sincere in their congratulations. They seemed to think that I had been a good choice and this meant the world to me. I looked across the room and saw the girl who had so wanted the award. Awkwardly, I walked toward her and said in as compassionate tone as I could something to the effect that it could have just as easily been her to receive the award. She put her hands on her hips, glared at me and said, "Don't send any hearts and flowers my way, girlie." During my entire time in grade school I don't think I had ever felt so sad for anyone before as I felt for that poor girl. I realized how very much she had wanted that recognition and I hoped that eventually she would have it.

WITH OUR TEXTBOOKS turned in and the room thoroughly cleaned, it was time for school to let out. We were dismissed for the last time from OLPH. Next year would be a new adventure. My older brother was heading to West Point. My younger brother would now be the oldest in the family at OLPH, and my sister would start first grade there. As for me, yes, I would be starting high school, but more important, I would be leaving behind forever my beloved Sisters of Charity of the Blessed Virgin Mary. The separation tugged at my heart and made me sad. This feeling was eventually replaced with gratitude. I will always be appreciative for the experience of having them present in my life at such a crucial time of my development. The first polite phrases I learned in my initial days of grade school become more poignant in light of my gratitude. ***Yes, Sister! Thank you, Sister!***

Epilogue

In the winter of 1964, the Beatles consumed the thoughts and conversations of my peers and me. I had study hall with the rest of the freshman girls. One afternoon, before we had settled into our seats, a girl gleefully said, "Did you hear what happened at OLPH yesterday?" All of us gathered around as she told a story of a group of parents forcing Sister Rupertine to back down from a stance she had taken. It seems that some of the eighth-grade girls decided to emulate the Beatles by cutting their hair in long bangs.

In Sister's opinion, they had gone too far and she thought their hair was shaggy and distracting. She ordered them to cut their bangs in such a way that their hair would be out of their eyes. The girls did not do this, and when Sister attempted to take stronger measures by calling their parents, her plan backfired. The parents informed Sister that they were in charge of their children and if the girls wanted to wear their hair that way, they would continue to have it that way.

The girls in my study hall cackled upon hearing this anecdote. I walked away feeling sad. I had trusted Sister Rupertine completely. I could not imagine resisting her guidance like that. Looking back, I feel that this time in our history was a turning point for many. Suddenly, Sister Rupertine was not regarded as a wise woman. Rather, from that time forward, she endured many criticisms. Now she was considered too old-fashioned. Her words lost their authority and were replaced with society's current idea of individual freedom. I perceived this in the reactions from my peers in study hall that day, and I was concerned.

At home that afternoon, I thought about this incident. And I remembered a day in eighth grade when Sister had taken the entire class over to the church. She told us that she wanted to talk to us and that her topic was so serious that she felt the church was the most appropriate place to discuss it. When we seated ourselves quietly in the pews, she began to talk about the privilege of having the Catholic faith. She referred to the early days of the Church and spoke of the martyrs. She told us that someday we too might be called to martyrdom, but she emphasized that she did not mean by this a physical sacrifice. She said it was much more likely that some of us might be called upon to be spiritual martyrs. For this reason, she urged us to become strong in all aspects of our spiritual lives.

I began to realize following the situation with the parents what Sister could have meant. I am certain that Sister Rupertine saw nothing wrong with the Beatles. Her complaint was against the flaunting of disrespect by the students who then received support from their parents. She was not worried about her own ego. She had the vision to see the far-reaching effects on the children and society. I believe that she had already seen this coming when she spoke to us that day in eighth grade.

Sister Rupertine was one of those spiritual martyrs. Her eyes revealed sorrow for the world, yet her heart revealed her trust in God and her love for her students. The same has been true for Mother Teresa, Pope John Paul II, as well as countless unknown people who have joined themselves with Christ to suffer for the world. Sister's exhortation to a strong spiritual life is timeless. Guiding us to think about that was her greatest gift to us. I am infinitely grateful for her efforts.

This gratitude stretches equally to the other women to whom this book is dedicated. Although I never experienced them in the classroom, Sisters St. Camillus, Honoria, Delrita, and Georgius each contributed to my growth. I extend my appreciation especially to those nuns who were my classroom teachers. Sister Carlice enthusiastically brought learning alive and made God's love tangible to me. Sister Mary St. Roche demonstrated by her example the qualities of loyalty and a quirky sense of humor perfectly suited to the mind of a third grader. In Sister Lena I found a call to excellence and a wonderful example of patient resignation in the face of the infirmities of aging. Sister Leonine was the embodiment of reserve, kindness, and quality. And finally, Sister Harold with her dry wit and no-nonsense attitude was wise beyond her years; to this day she continues to amaze me.

In my own years as an educator and as a parent of children in school, I have been privy to many conversations regarding the particular "personality" of one class or another. Examples range from "This bunch has a wild streak," to "This is the brightest class of my career." The remarks have never been intended to limit a particular group or an individual within that class. Rather, they reflect a hallmark quality of that group. I feel that this same concept of personality can be applied to religious orders. Presumably, members of all religious orders demonstrate great faith. The Sisters of Charity of the Blessed Virgin Mary certainly did this, but the personality trait I identified with more than any other was their practicality. Combined with the foundation of faith they provided, this practicality is what I have carried with me throughout my life. Their example has demonstrated for me the pragmatic essence of the Gospel message. It led me to my discovery of the writings of Saint John of the Cross and Saint Teresa of Avila. Finally, it revealed to me the pure logic of regarding our Creator as our perfect Father and, as such, his accessibility to each of us.

It would be impossible to separate my gratitude toward my beloved teachers from my appreciation for my own parents. My parents did much more than just sacrifice financially to send their four children to Catholic schools. Each day, they themselves were living examples of the faith. They consistently supported the efforts of the nuns whether in their actions or in their remarks. Their relationship with my teachers created a circle of appreciation within me. I grew up a child of privilege. I was privileged to be Catholic, privileged to have faith-filled parents, and privileged to have remarkable teachers who served as beacons for my future.

Made in the USA
Lexington, KY
04 September 2012